FREE FORM CHIP CARVING PATTERNS

Carol A. Ponte

This book is lovingly dedicated to my Lord and Savior, Jesus Christ, and to my husband, Alfred M. Ponte, my teacher and source of inspiration.

1996 edition published by
Fox Chapel Publishing,
Box 7948,
Lancaster, PA 17604–7948.

Cover photography by Richard Hertzler

CONTENTS

An Introduction to Free Form Chip Carving

Free form chip carving has to be the easiest type of wood carving, and a good way for a beginner to get into the great hobby of carving. This form of carving is simply a matter of incising into the wood two lines in the opposite direction and in most cases connecting them with a short cut at the bottom.

First select a piece of wood (preferably basswood) on which the picture you wish to carve will fit nicely. Then sand the surface of the wood with a fine-grain sandpaper. After you wipe away the excess grit, trace the picture onto the board using carbon paper. Place the carbon paper, carbon side down, directly on the surface of the wood. Place the picture on top of the carbon paper and trace along the lines with a pencil or other pointed object. Try not to put excess pressure on the carbon paper with your fingers or the heel of your hand; you will leave smudges of carbon behind on the wood.

The photographs and brief descriptions below will give you an introduction to free form chip carving. Try several practice pieces and then choose one of the patterns in this book to try chip carving for yourself.

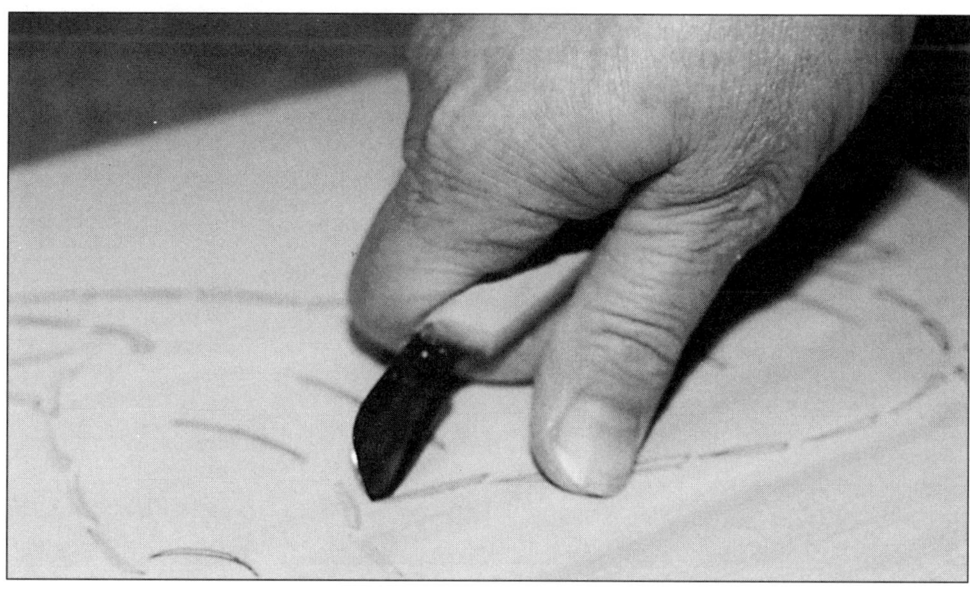

Hold the chip carving knife in your hand as shown in the picture. Use your thumb as a guide. The knuckle of your index finger should be anchored firmly on the wood. This will allow you to keep the same degree of an angle and depth as you carve into the wood.

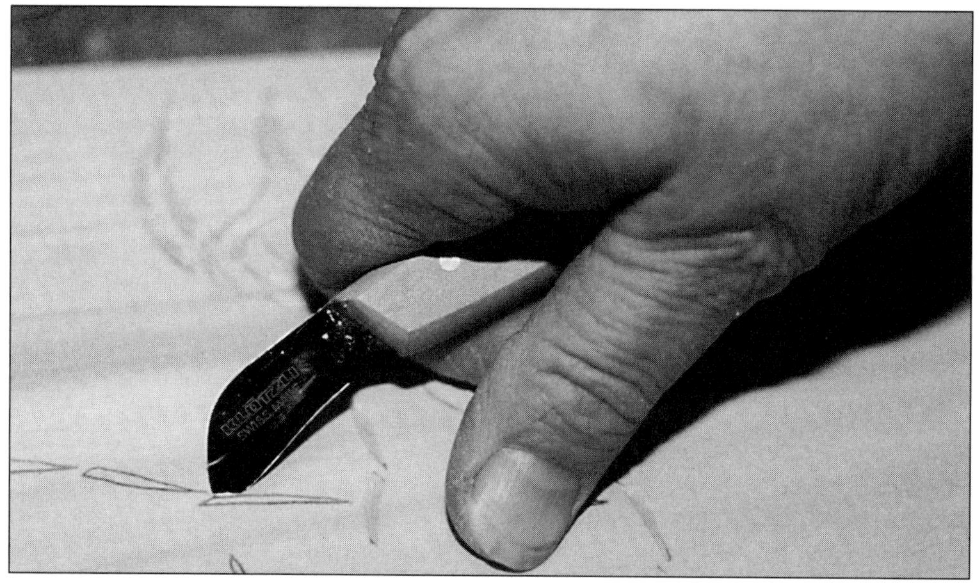

Starting at the point of the three lines, insert the point of the knife into the wood and draw the knife downward using more pressure as the space between the lines widens. Turn your work around 180 degrees and reverse depth cut along the opposite line.

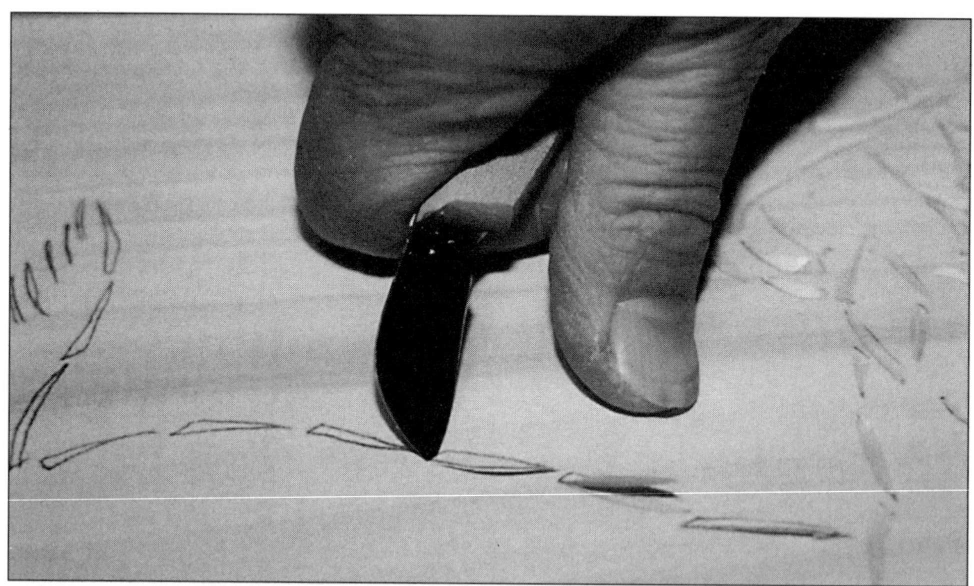

After some practice, you can repeat the down stroke on several lines before turning the work around 180 degrees and then do the opposite side of the elongated triangle. After the two lines are cut, then cut the connecting line at the same angle as you cut the two longer lines. The chip should pop right out.

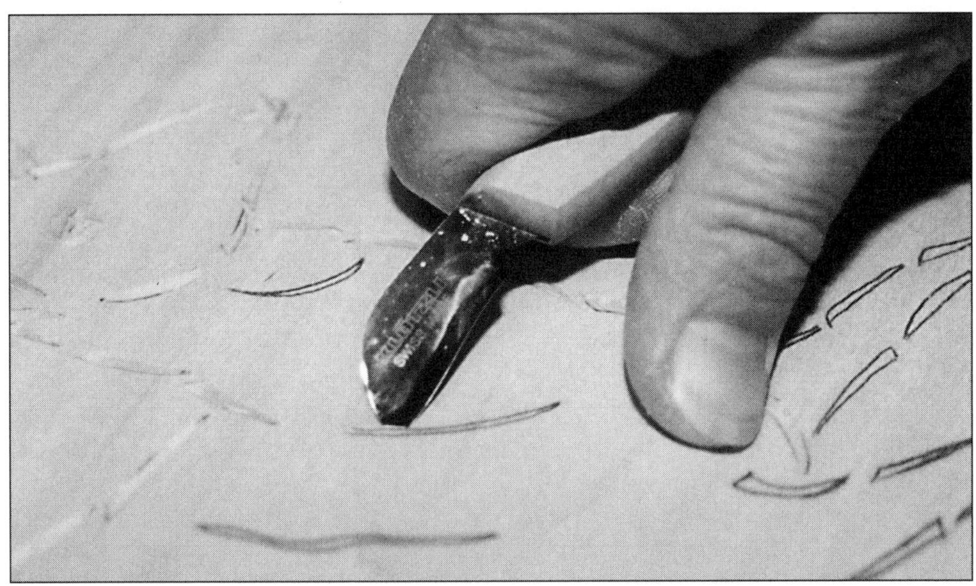

When starting a line, keep the knife moving constantly without lifting it out of the wood until you come to the end of the cut. If the knife is removed and positioned back into the cut, it is extremely difficult to have the knife land in the exact same place, therefore, two levels are made in the same cut.

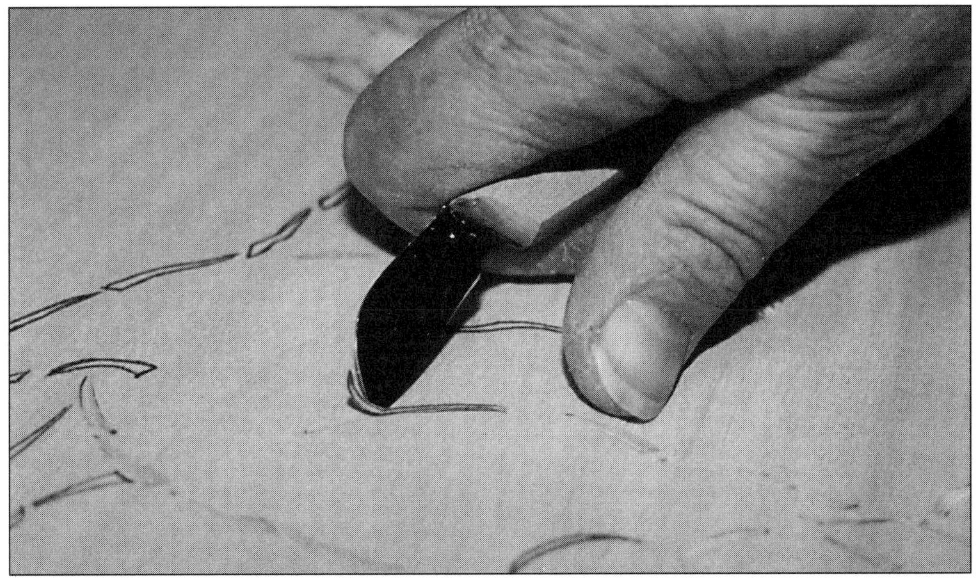

Do not erase any carbon lines left on the work (if you didn't cut close enough to remove the line) as it will burnish the wood and it will not accept stain as well. Rather, use a fine grain sandpaper and lightly sand with the grain of the wood. Remove the grit from the cuts with a soft tooth brush.

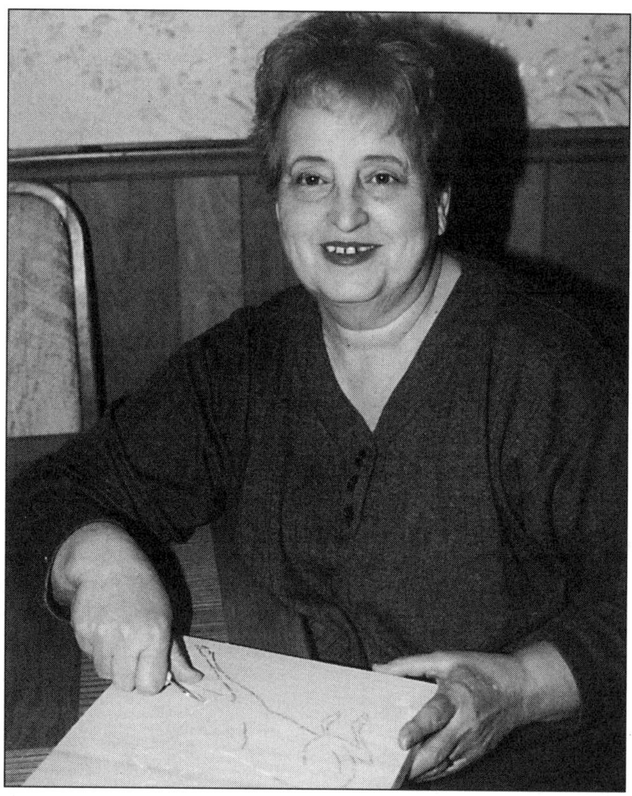

Using a nut pick sharpened to a point, score the very bottom of the cut where the two walls meet, forming the bottom of the V. This is to burnish or close up the mark left by the knife. When the project is completed, I like to use a stain that already has a wax mix in it. Then I buff it with a bristle brush on a drill.

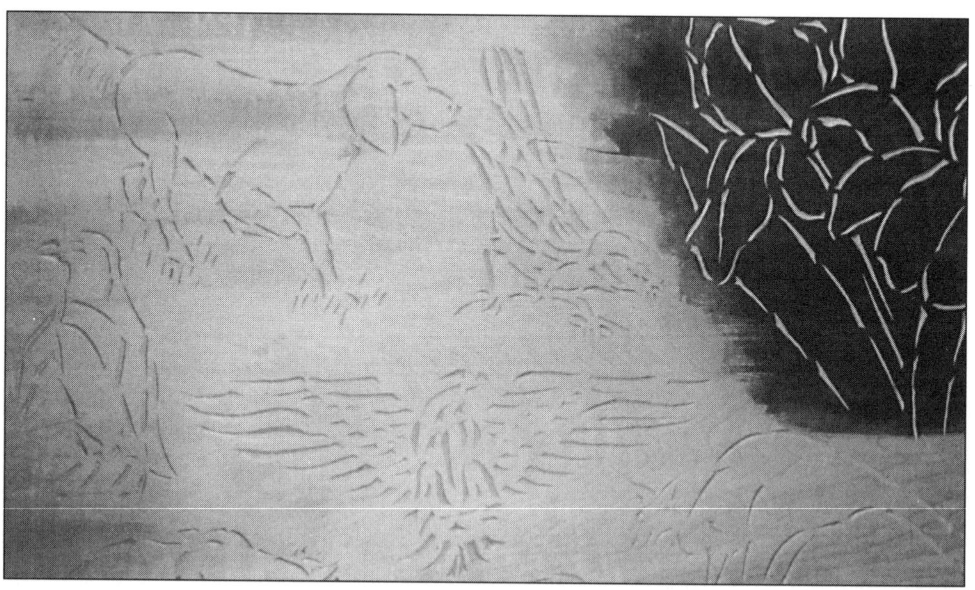

I like to apply the stain with a soft cloth that is dipped into the stain and then wrung out almost dry. Lightly lay the cloth onto a portion of the wood that has no cuts in it and quickly drag it across the piece going with the grain of the wood. Let the stain dry and apply it again 5 or 6 times. Some stain may get into the grooves, but it can be cut out with a fine slice from the knife. Then buff the piece with a soft bristle brush on a wheel.

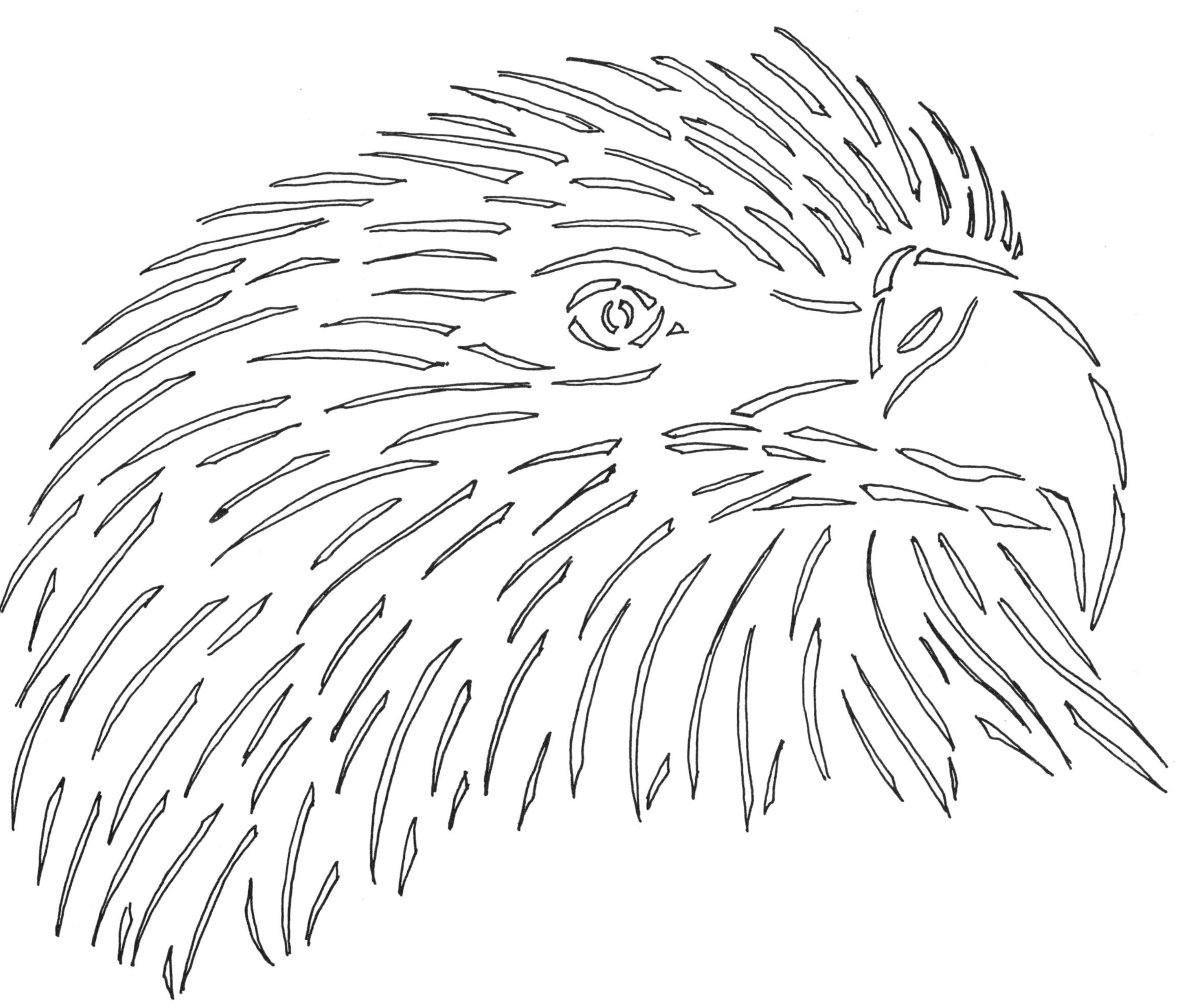

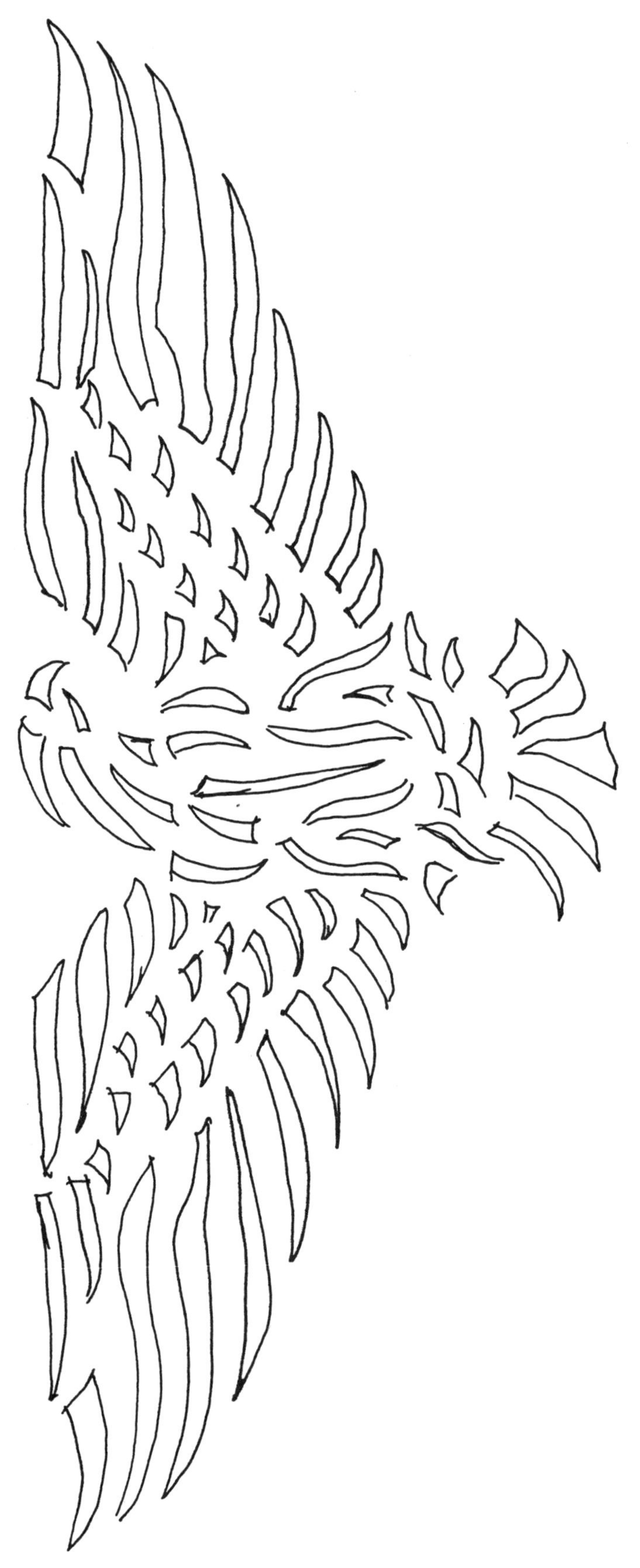

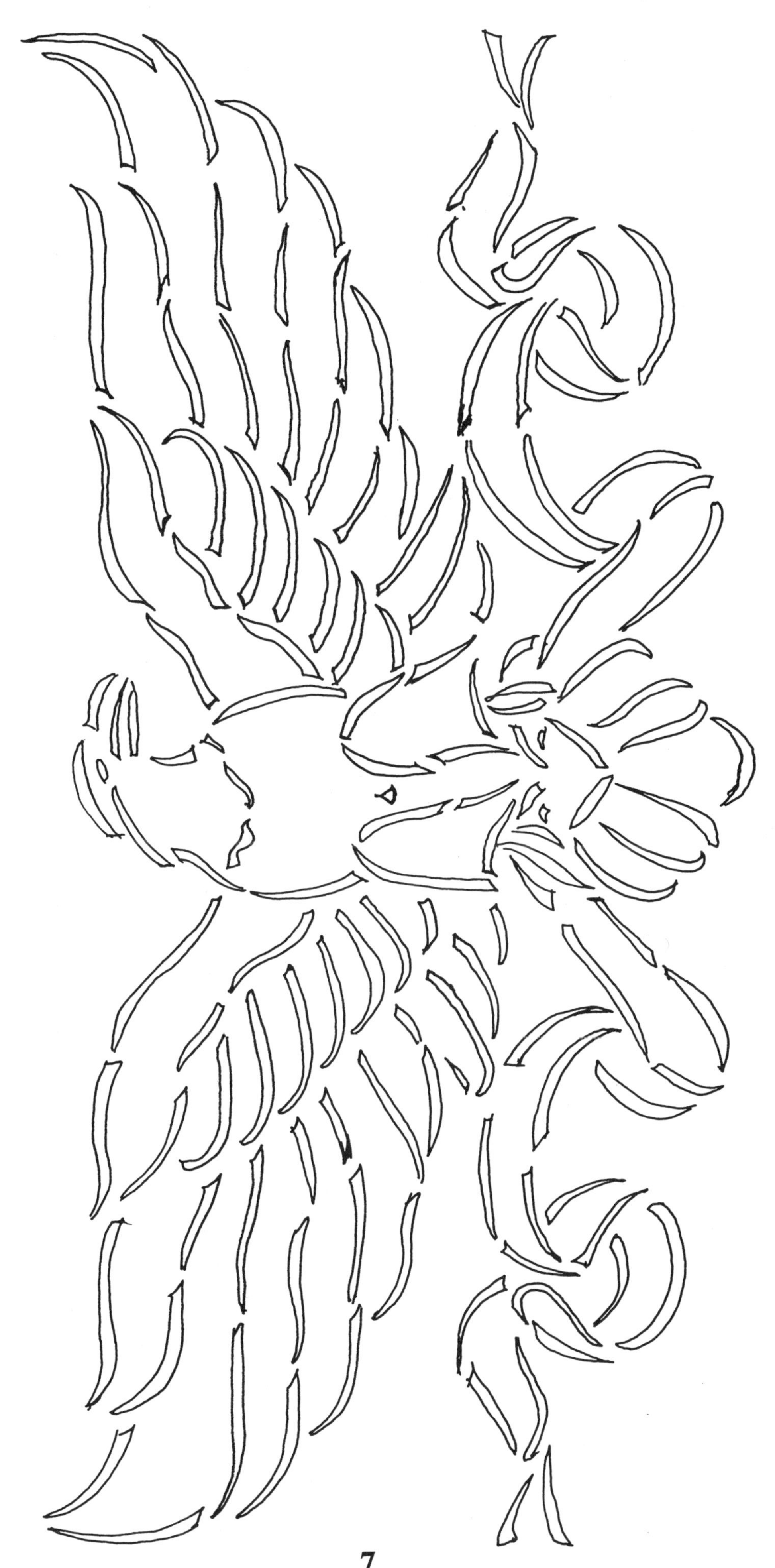

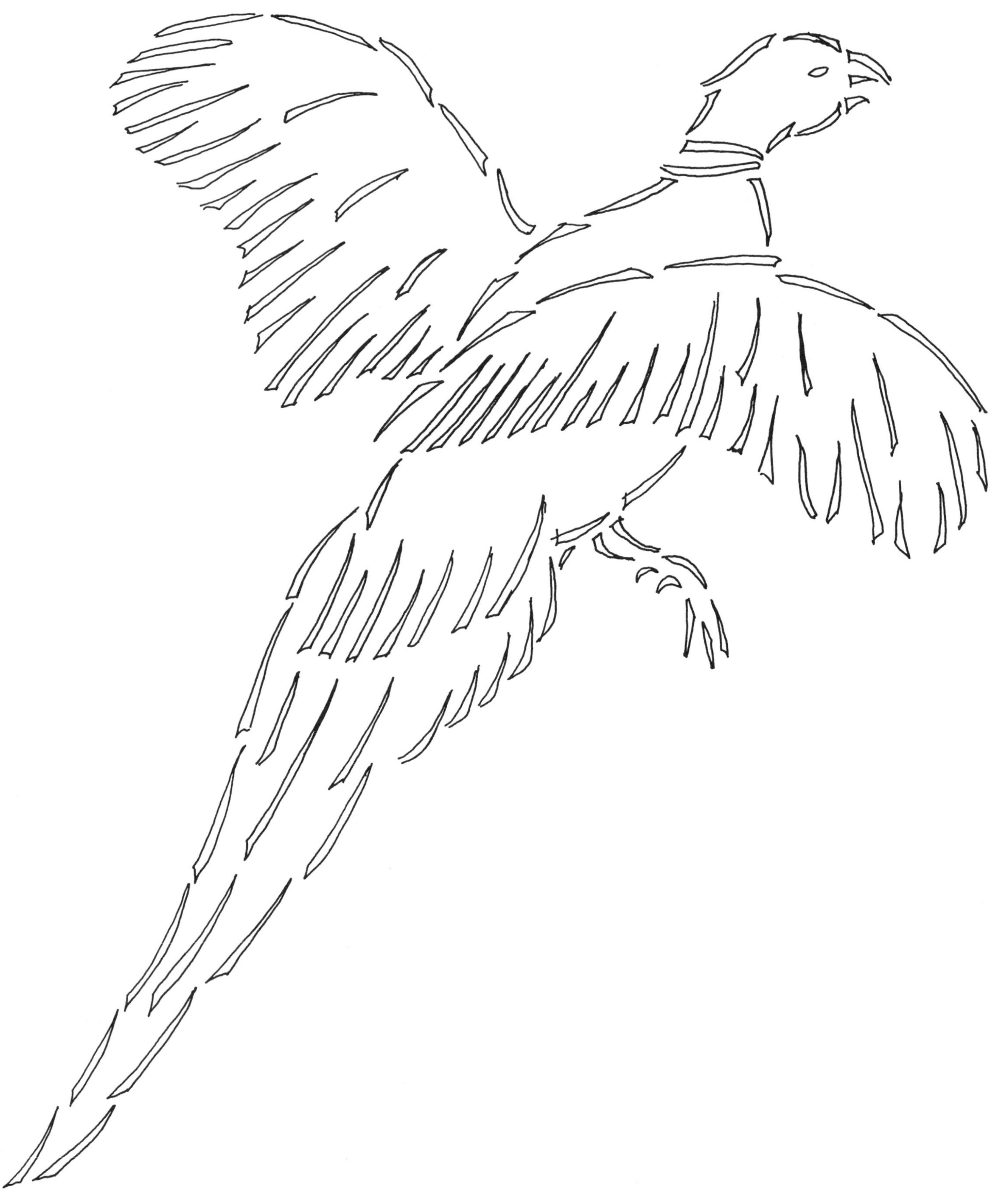

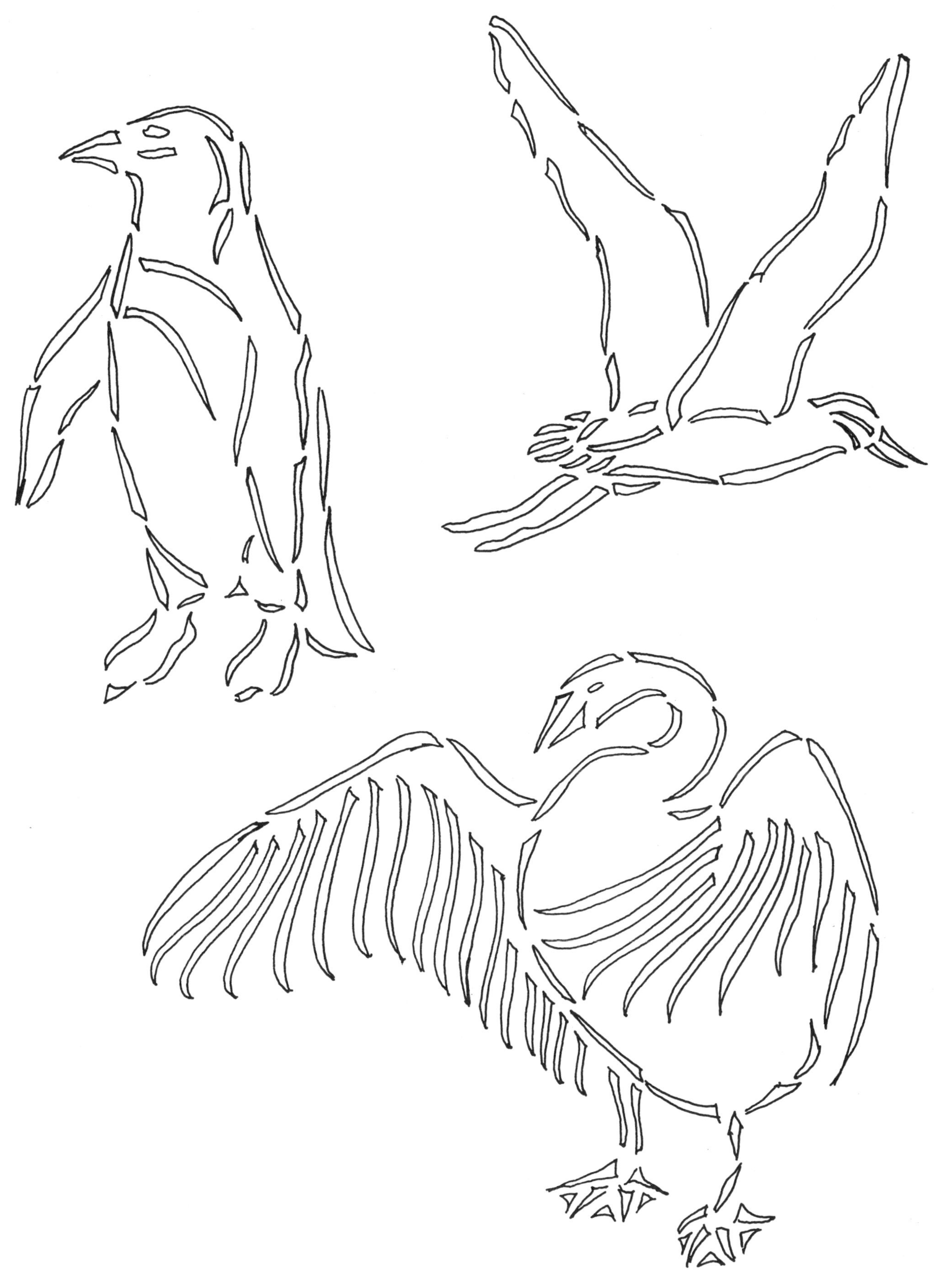

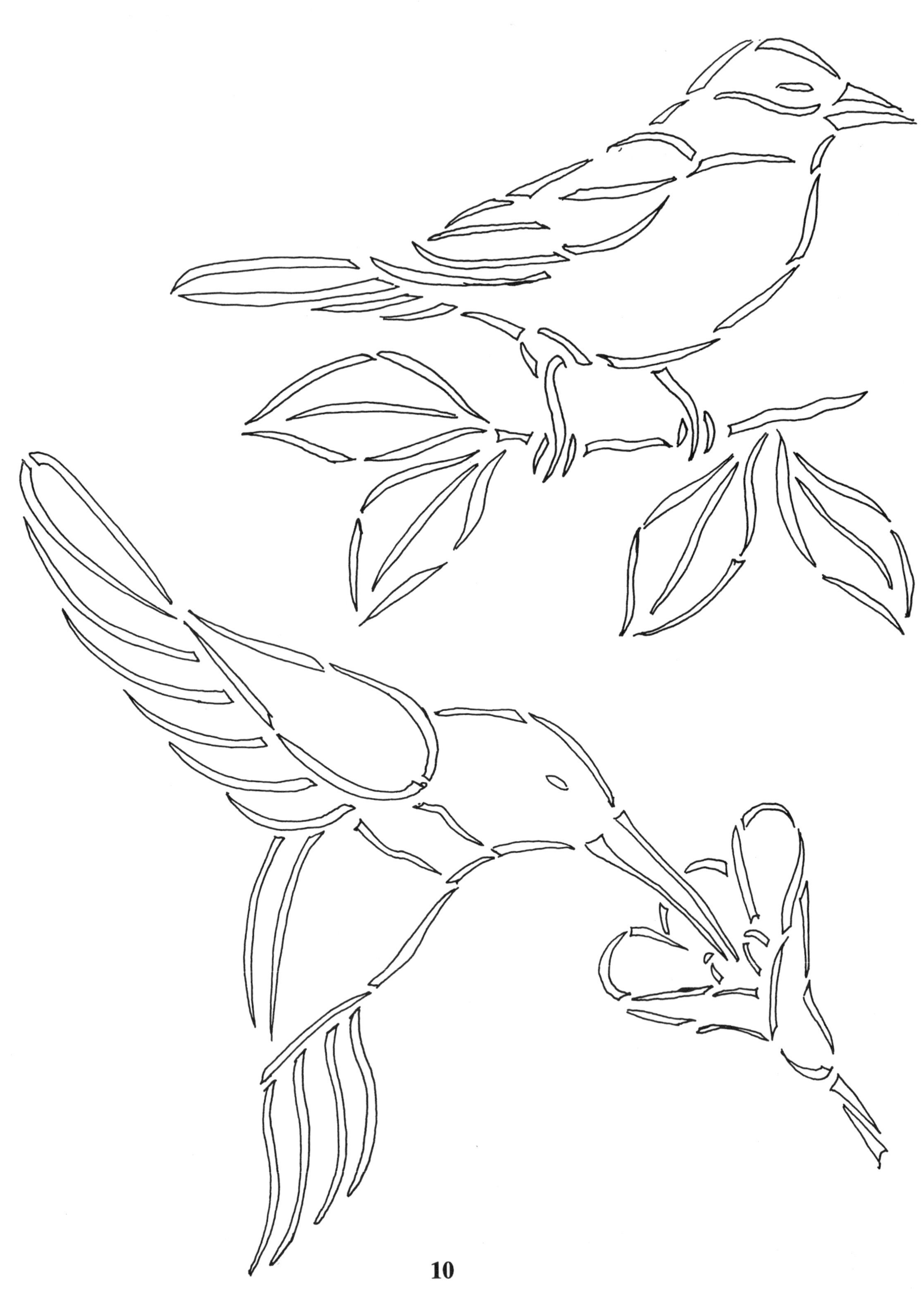

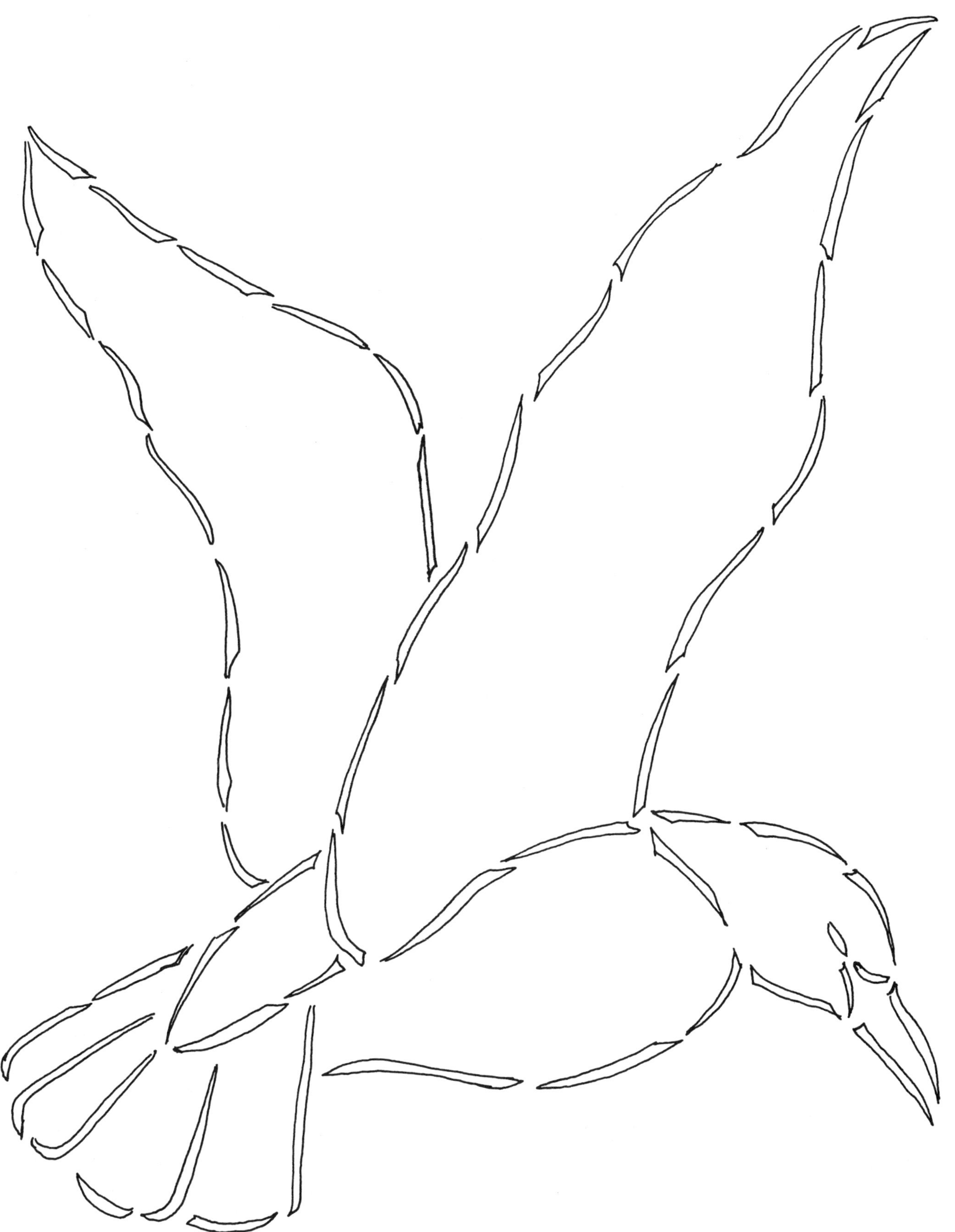

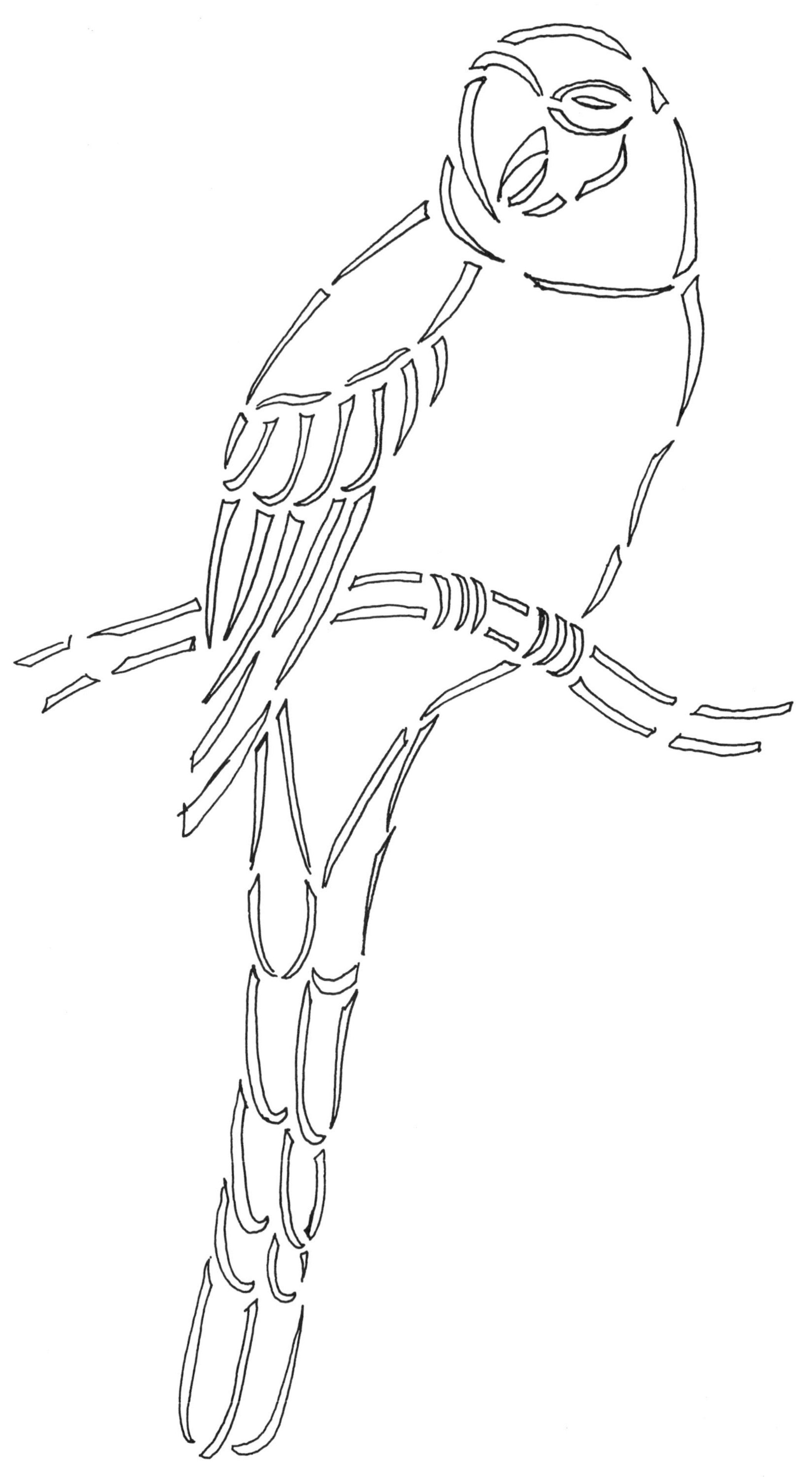

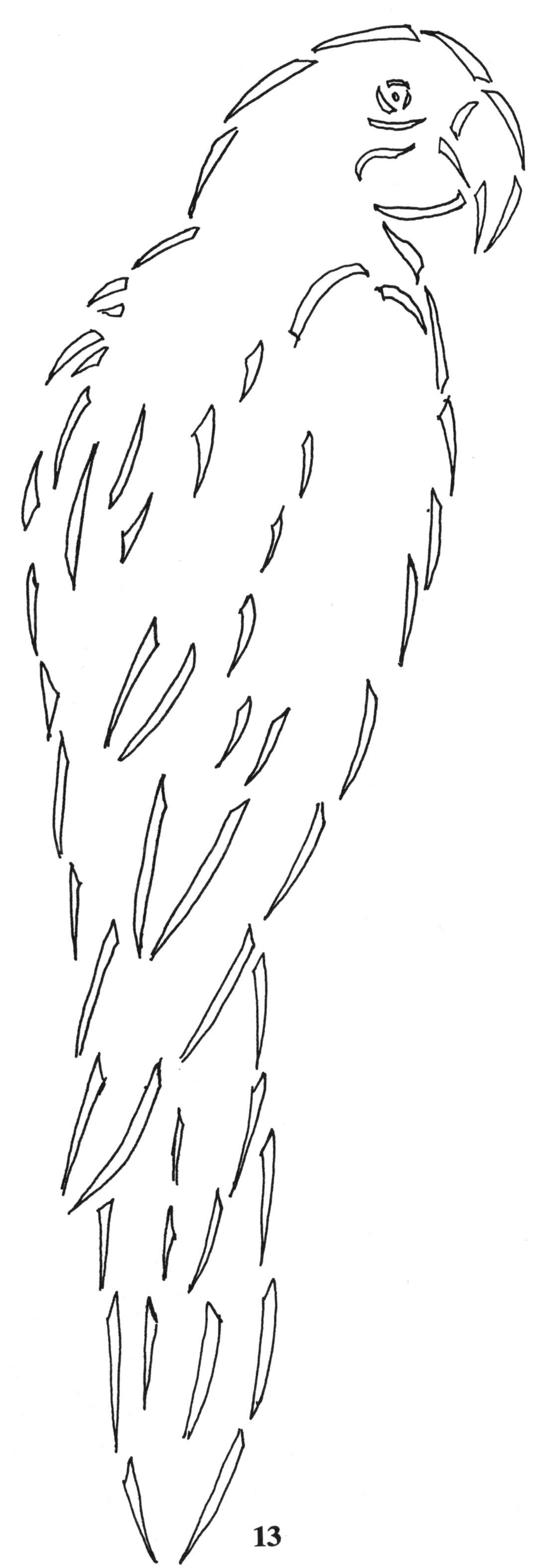

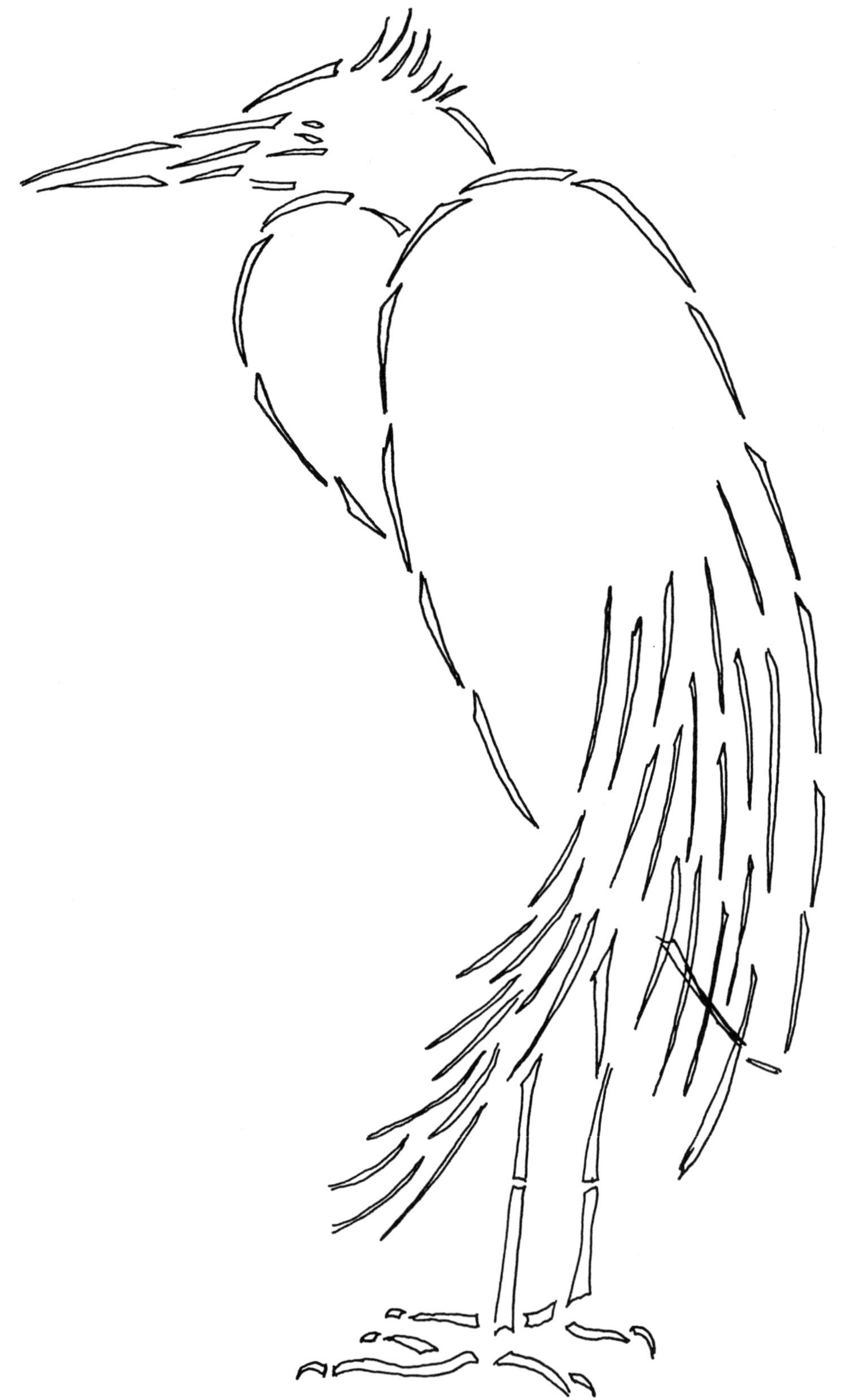

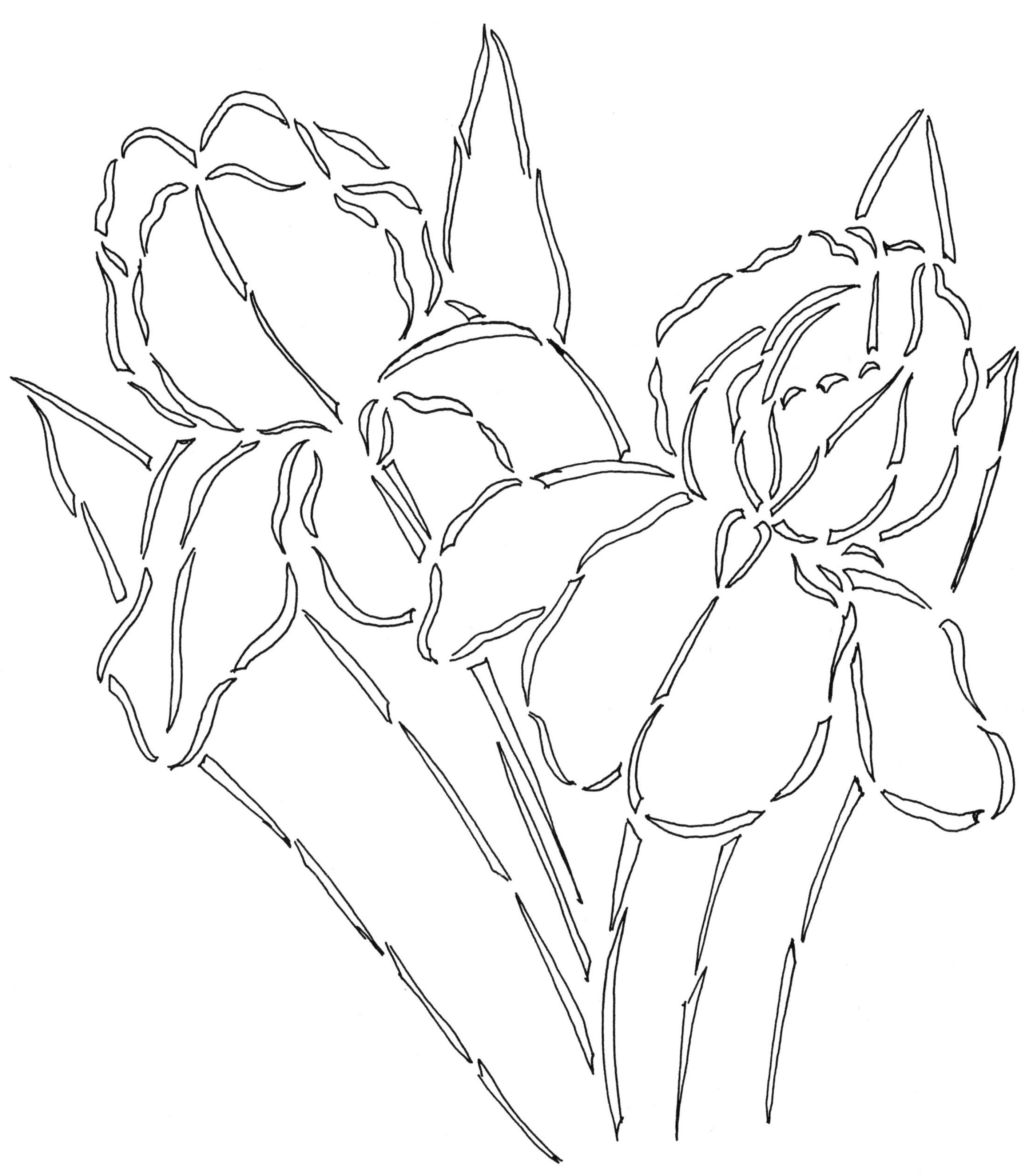

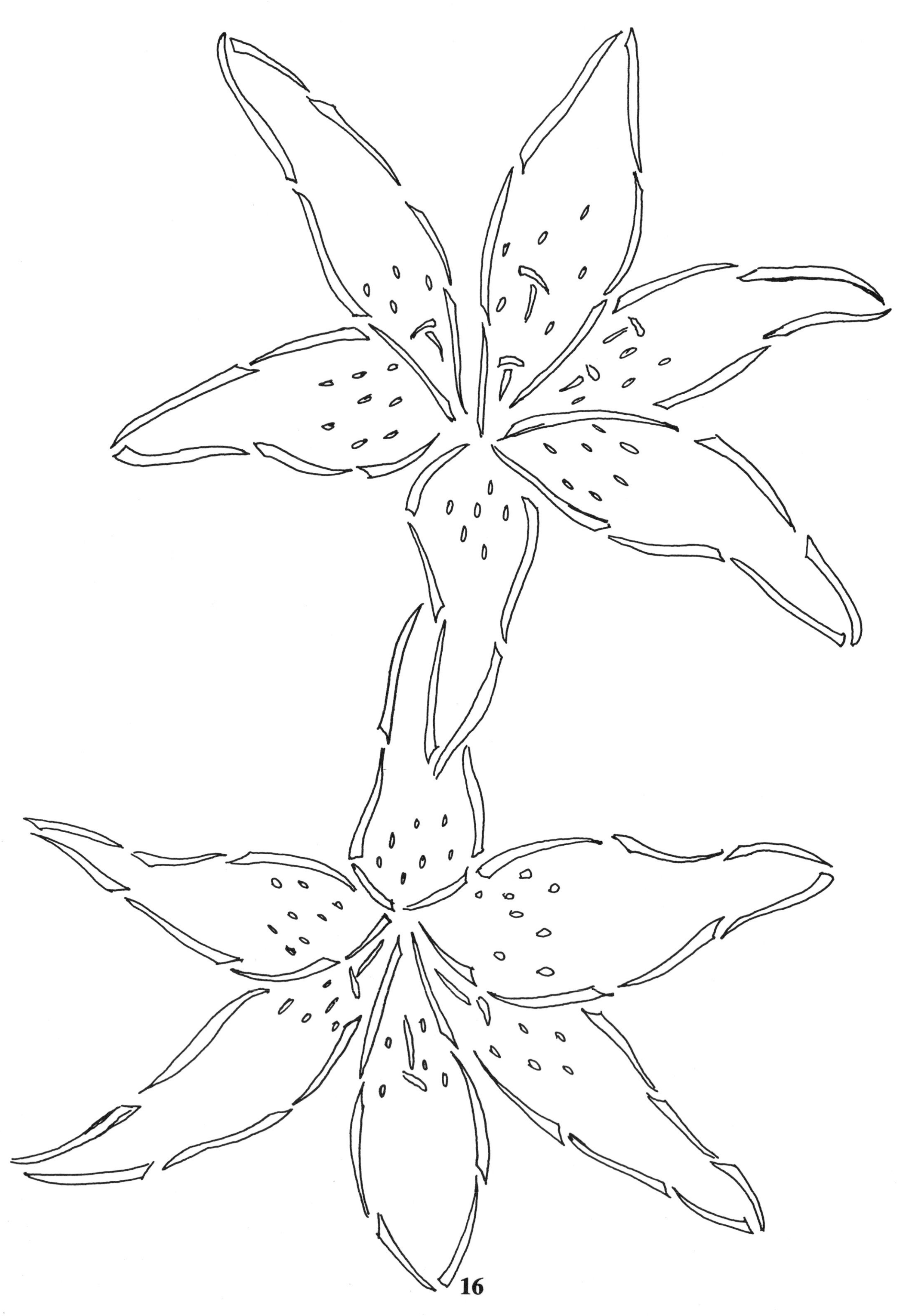

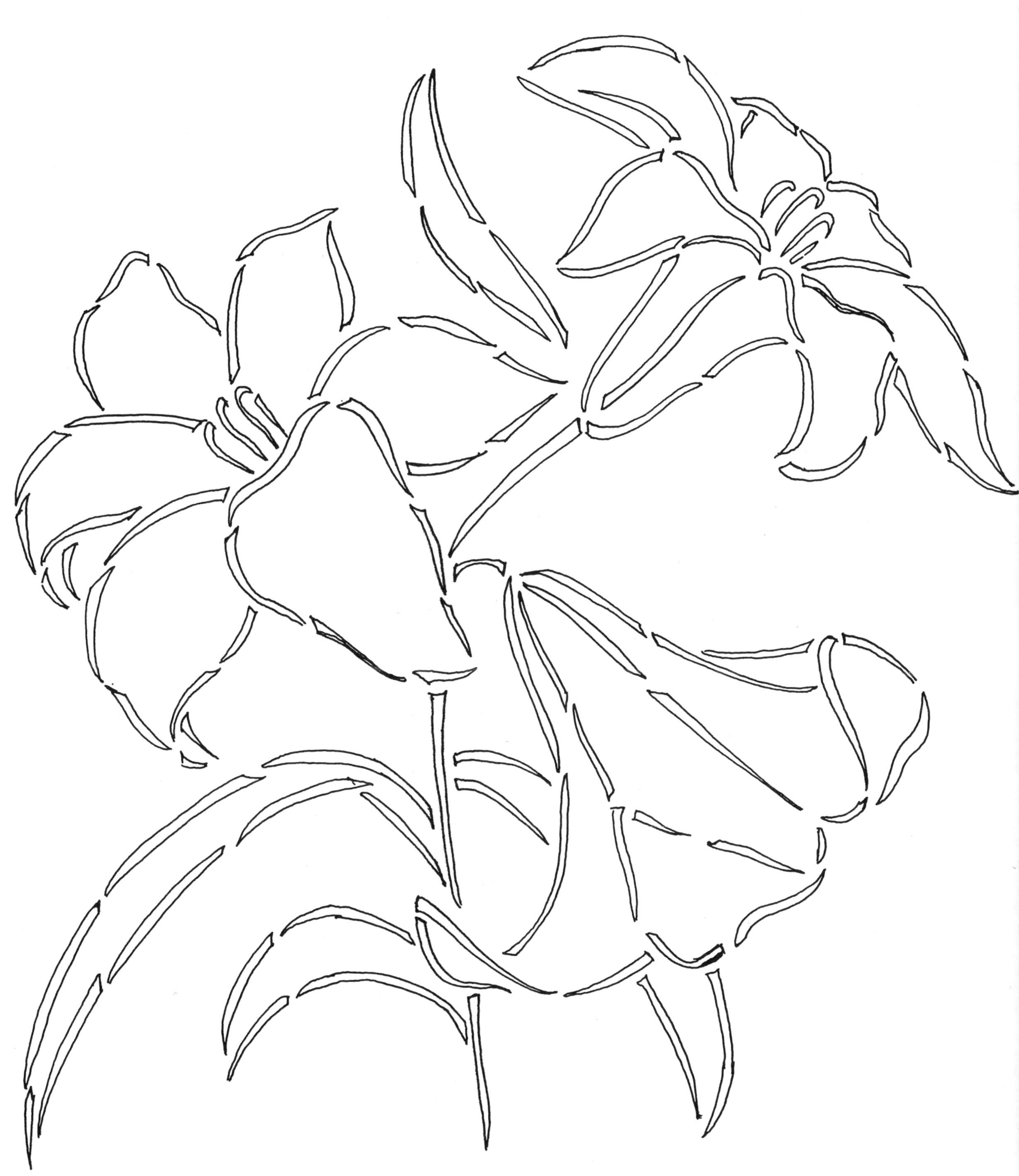

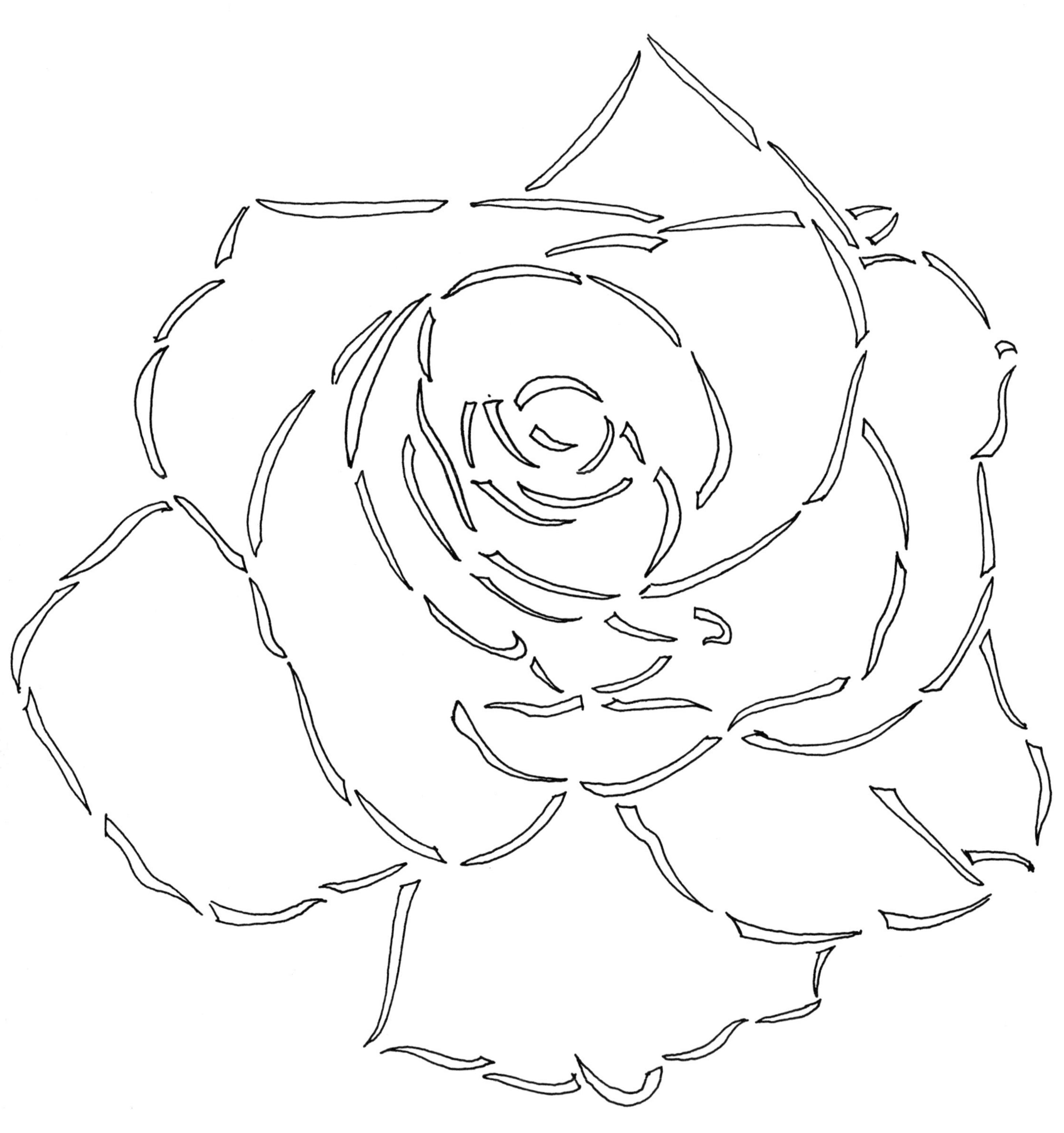

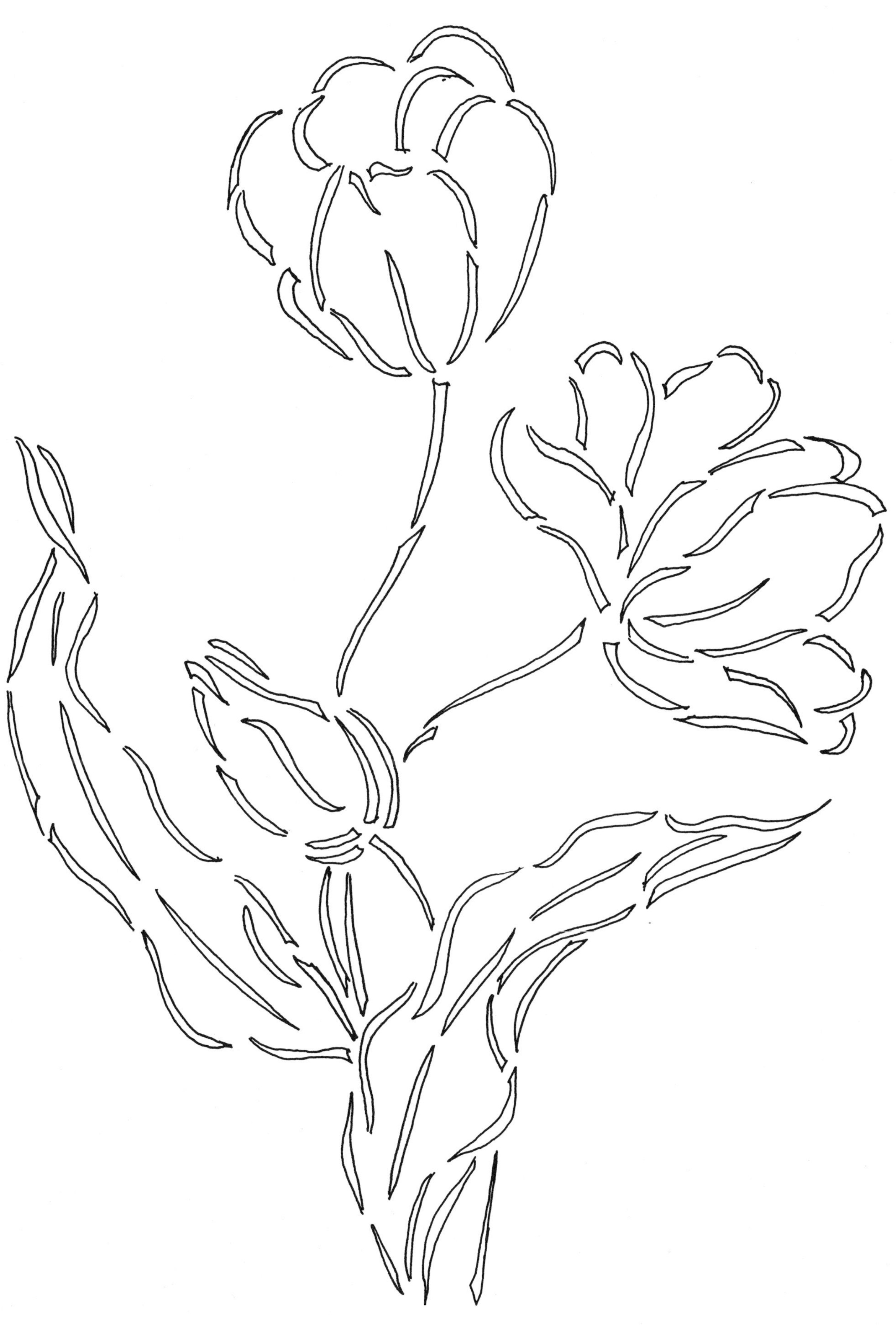

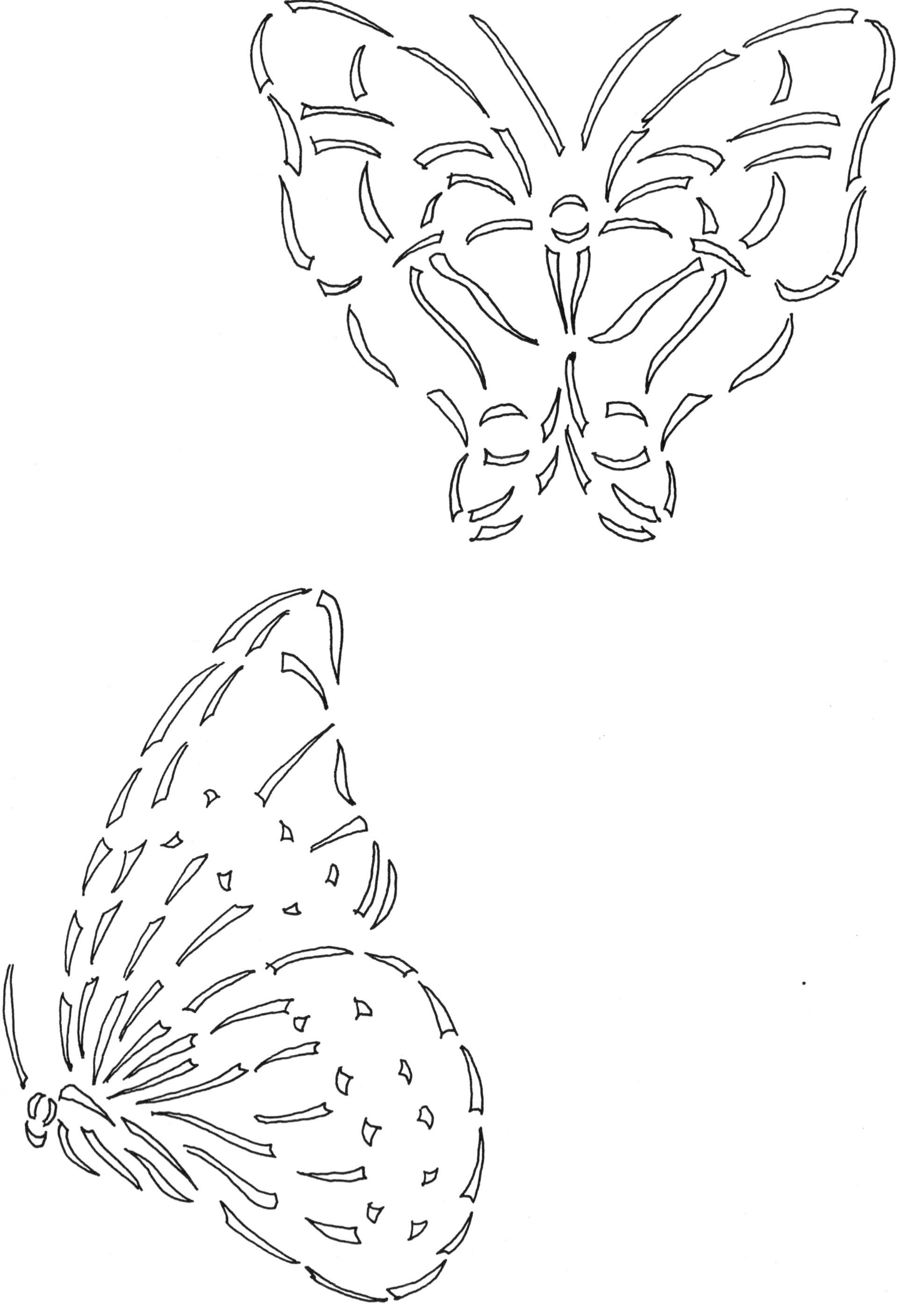

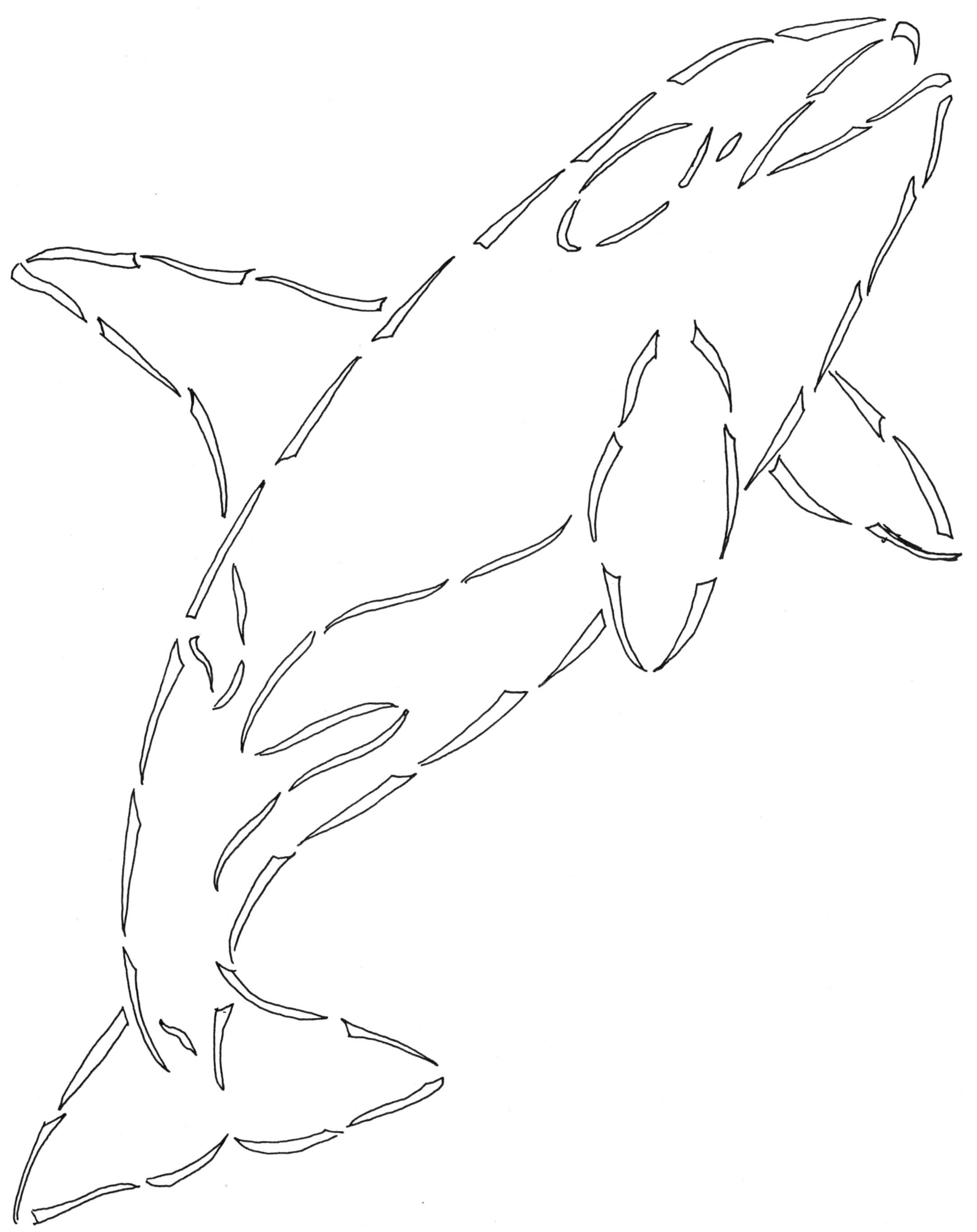

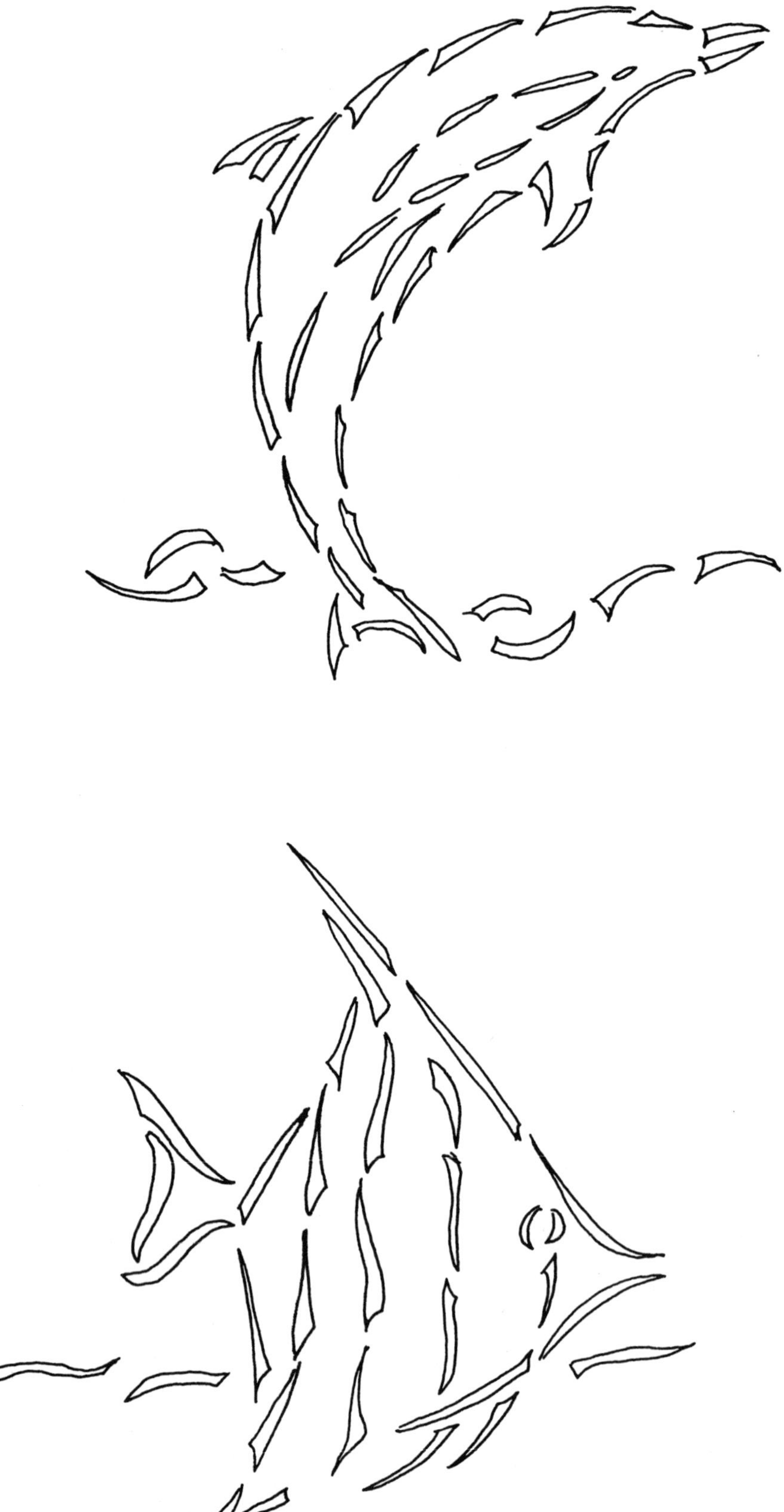

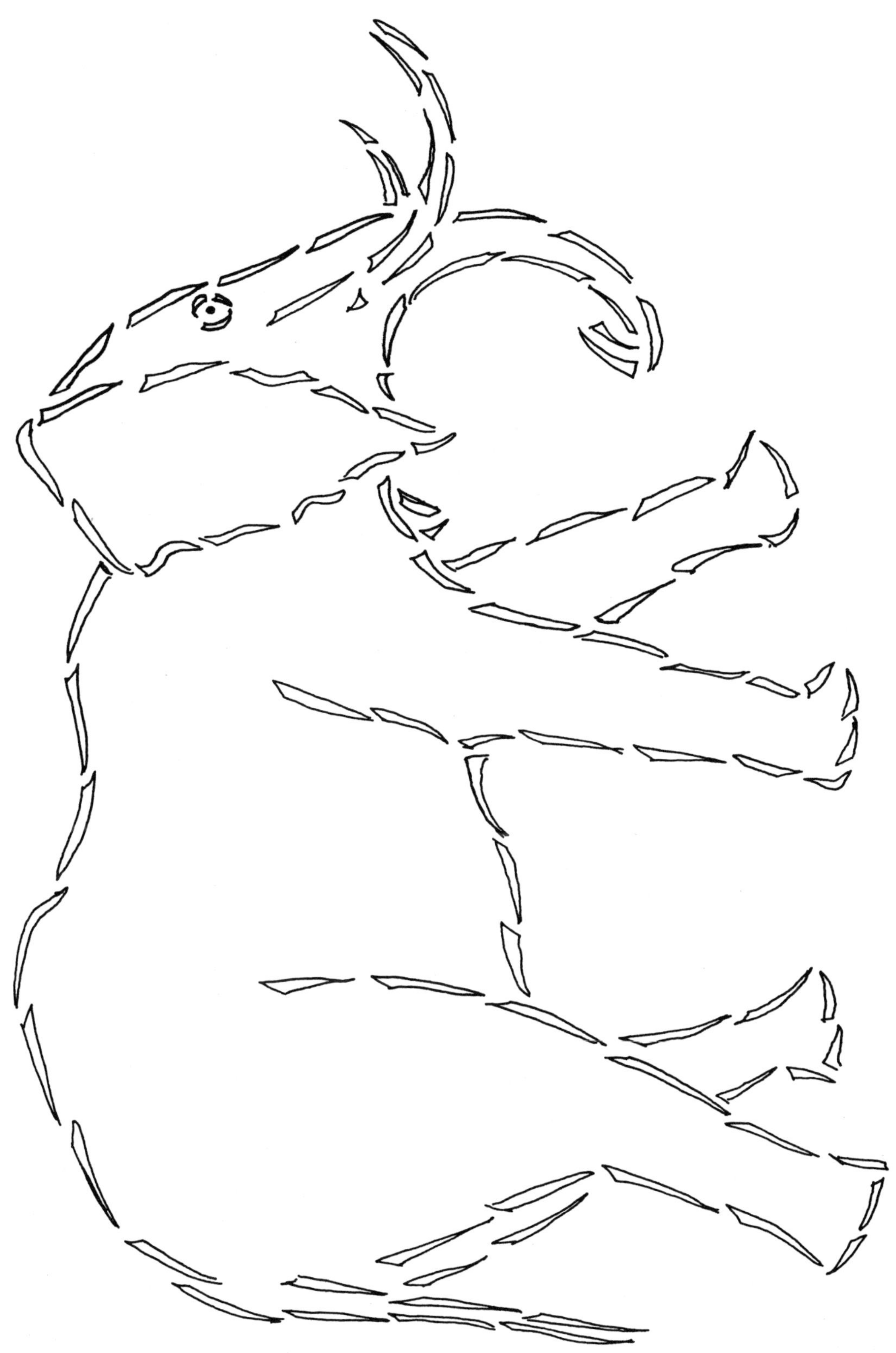

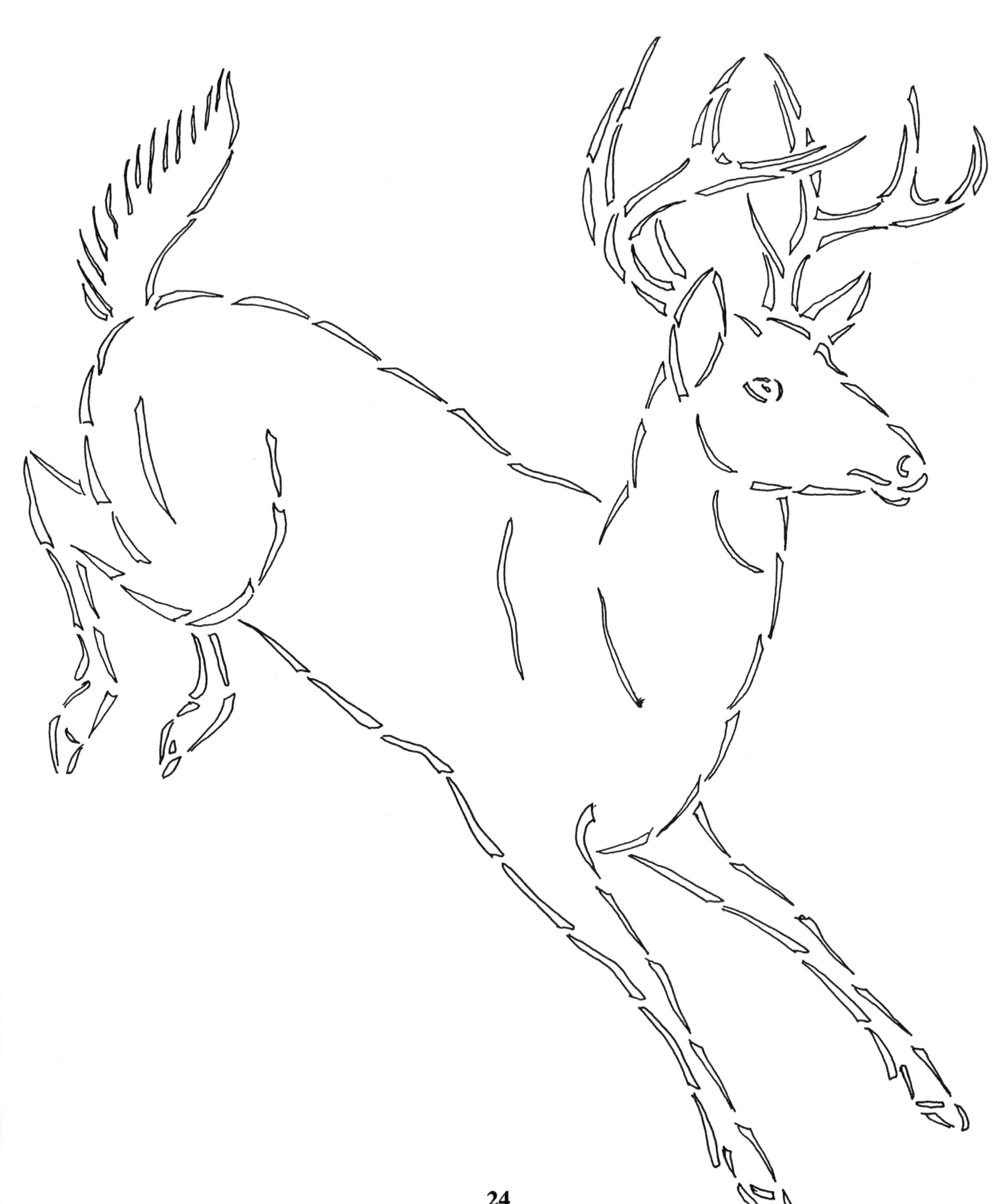

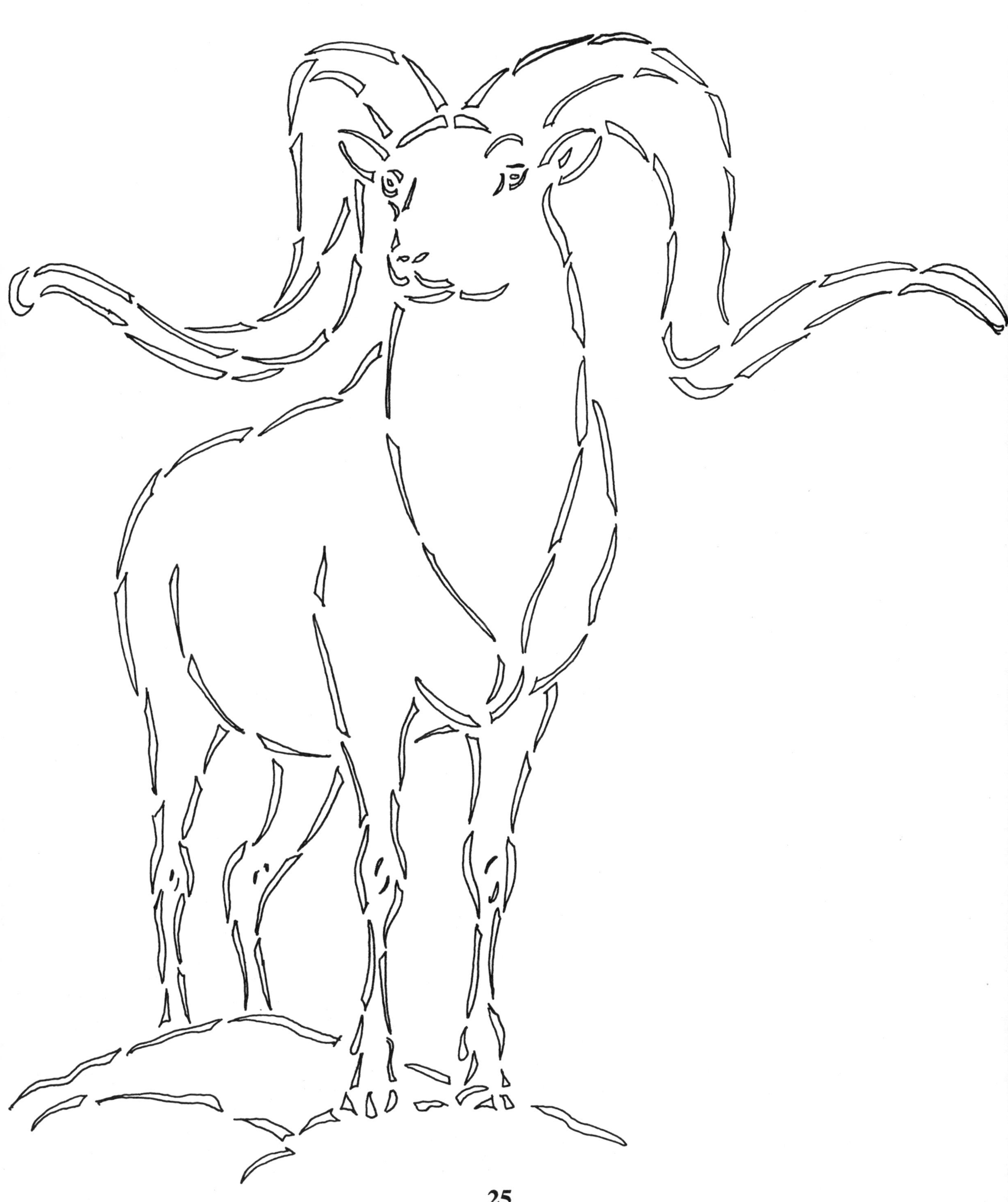

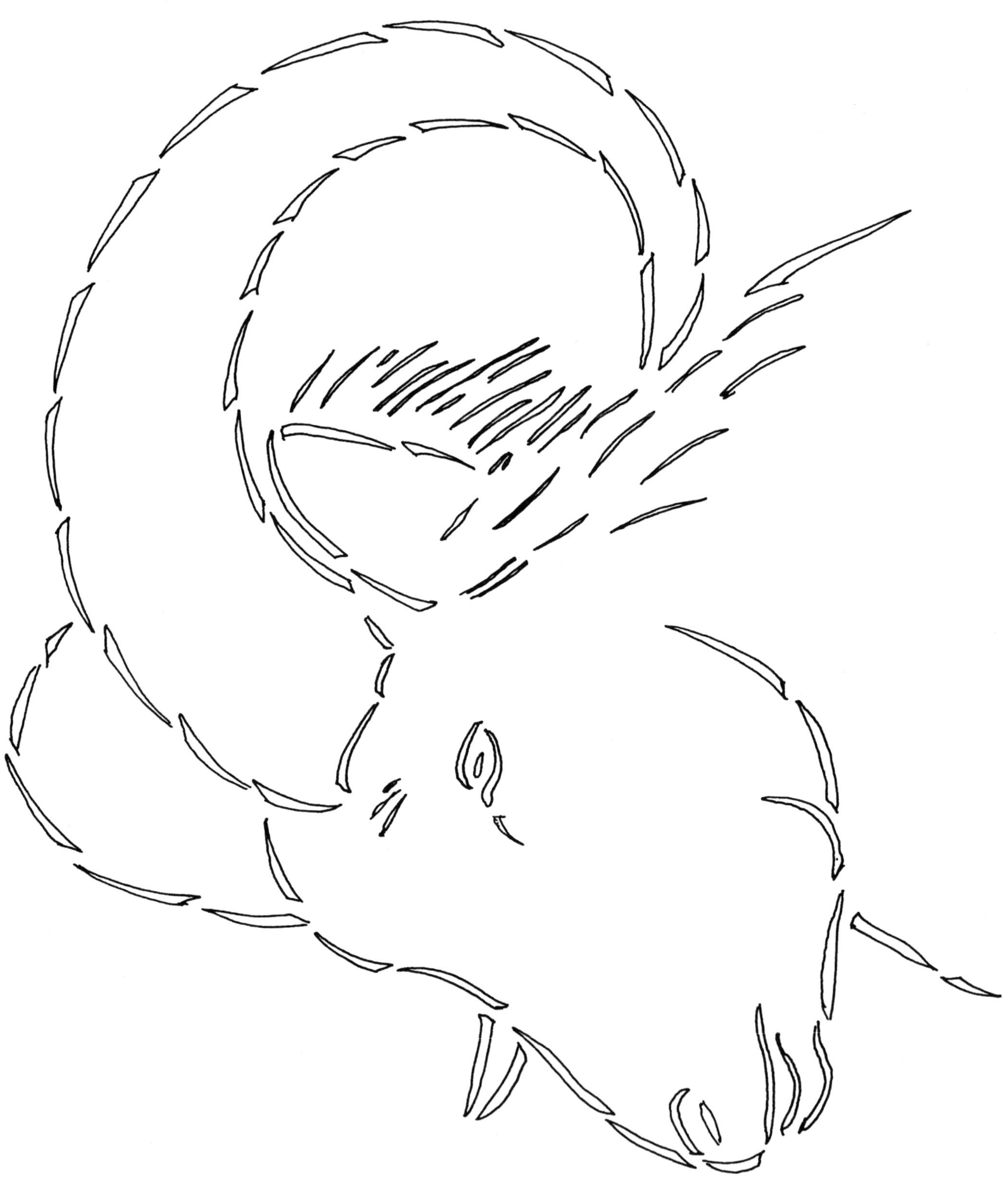

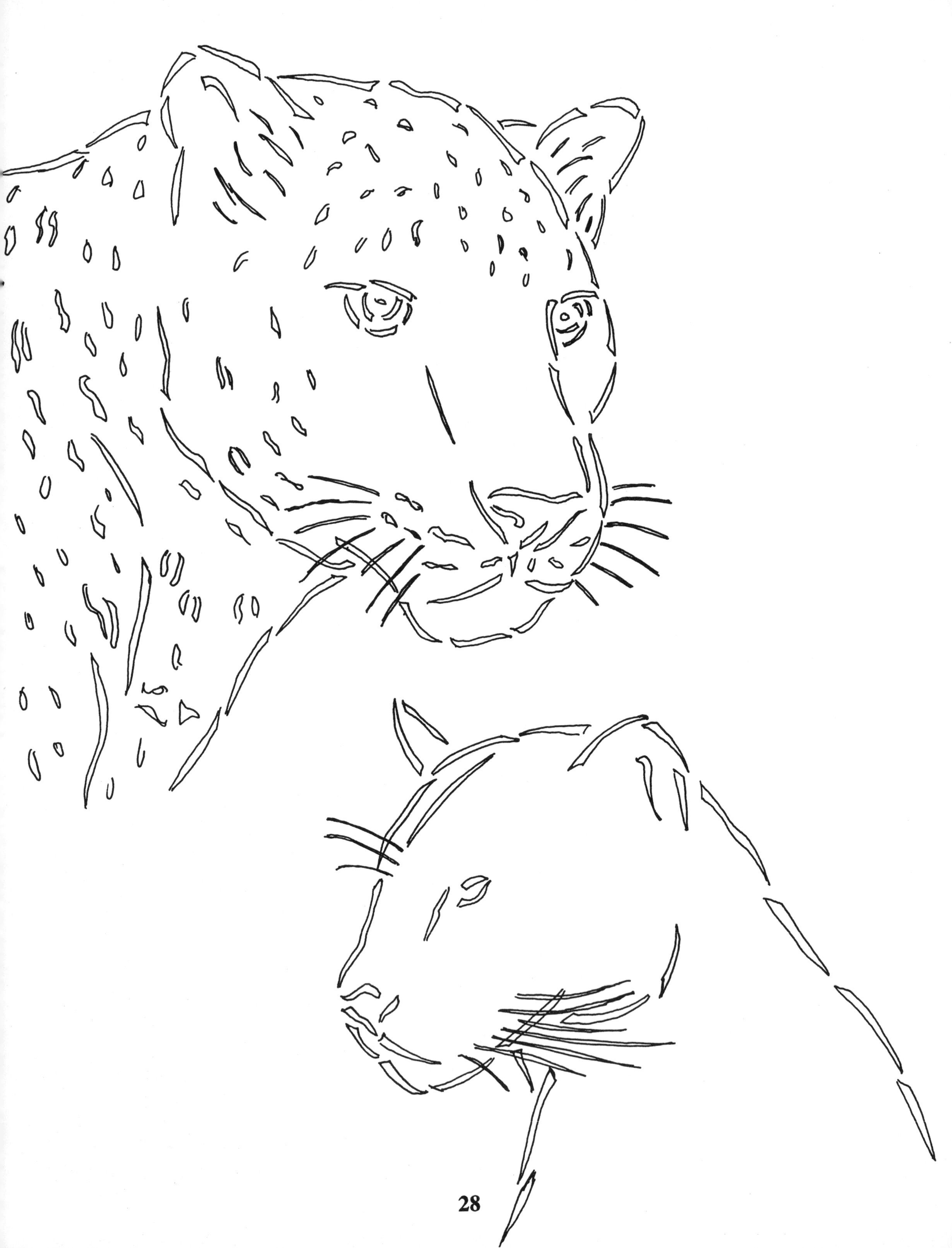

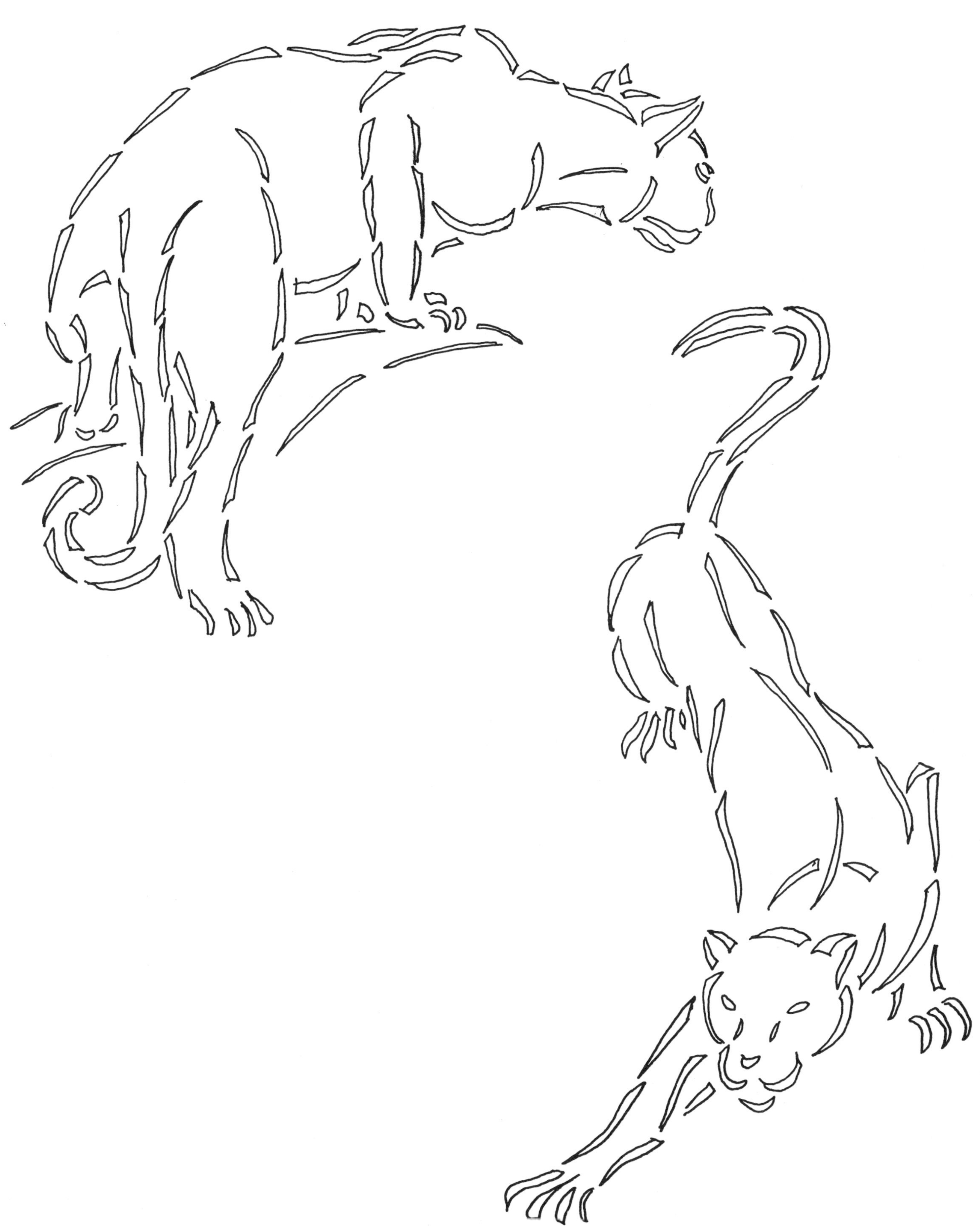

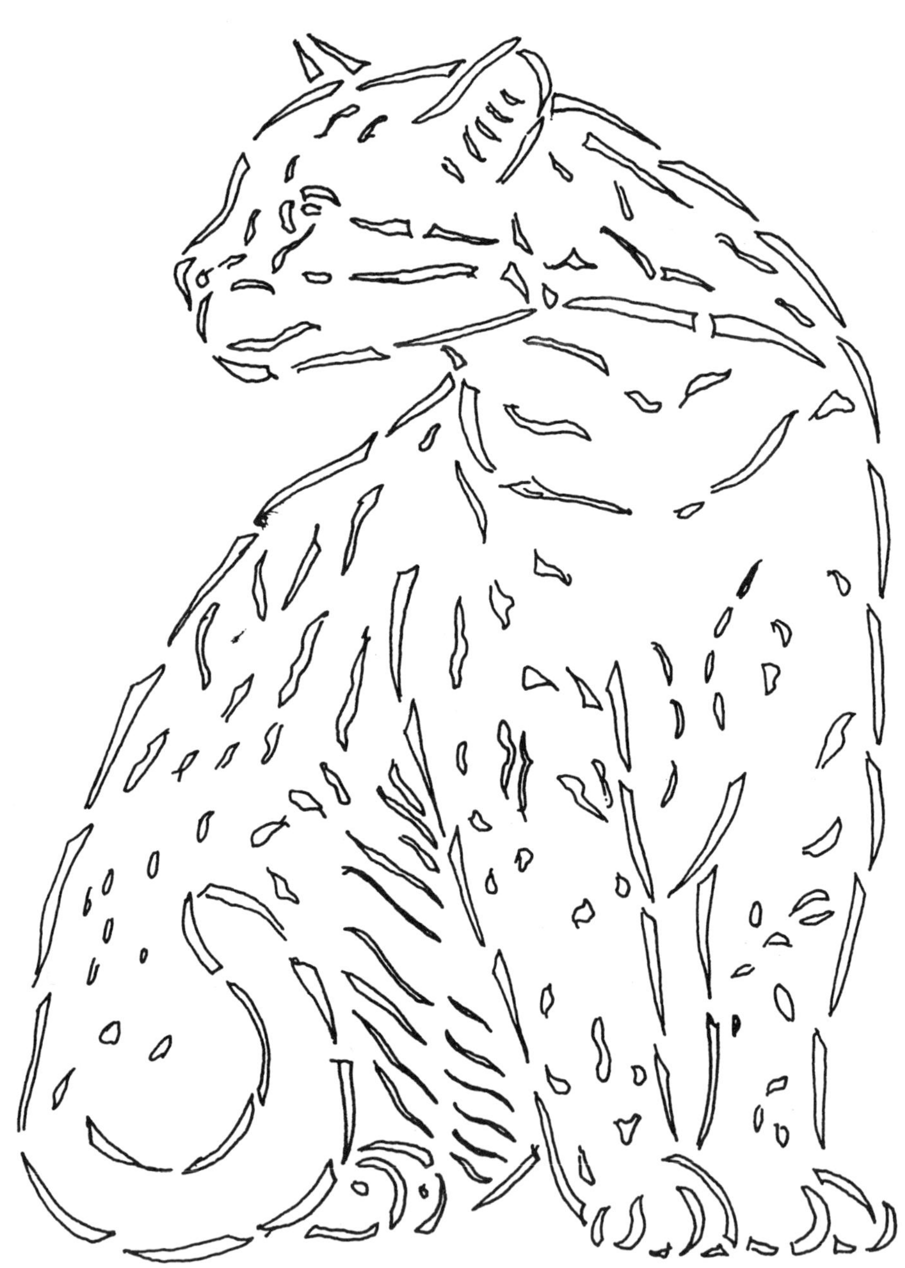

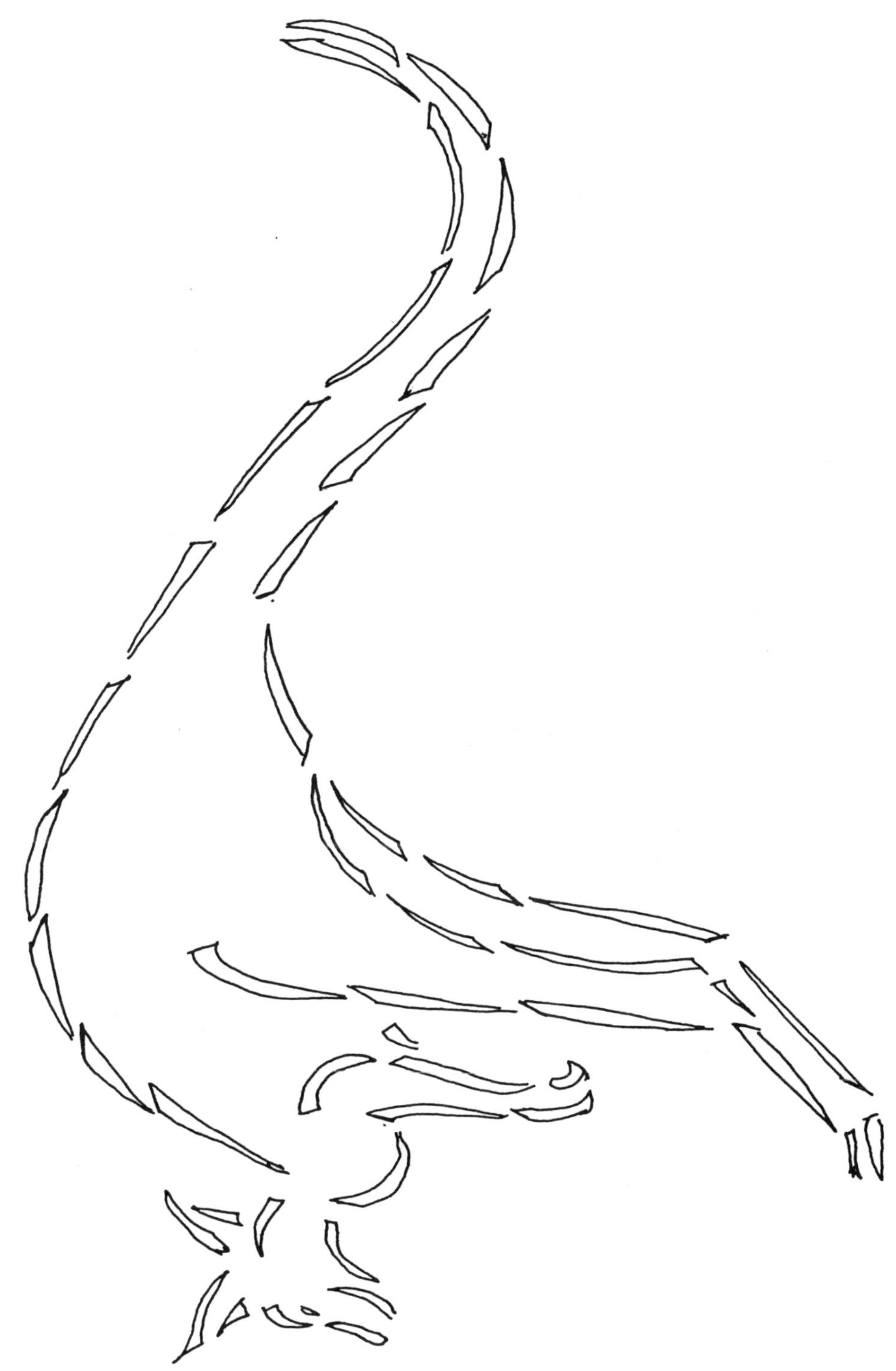

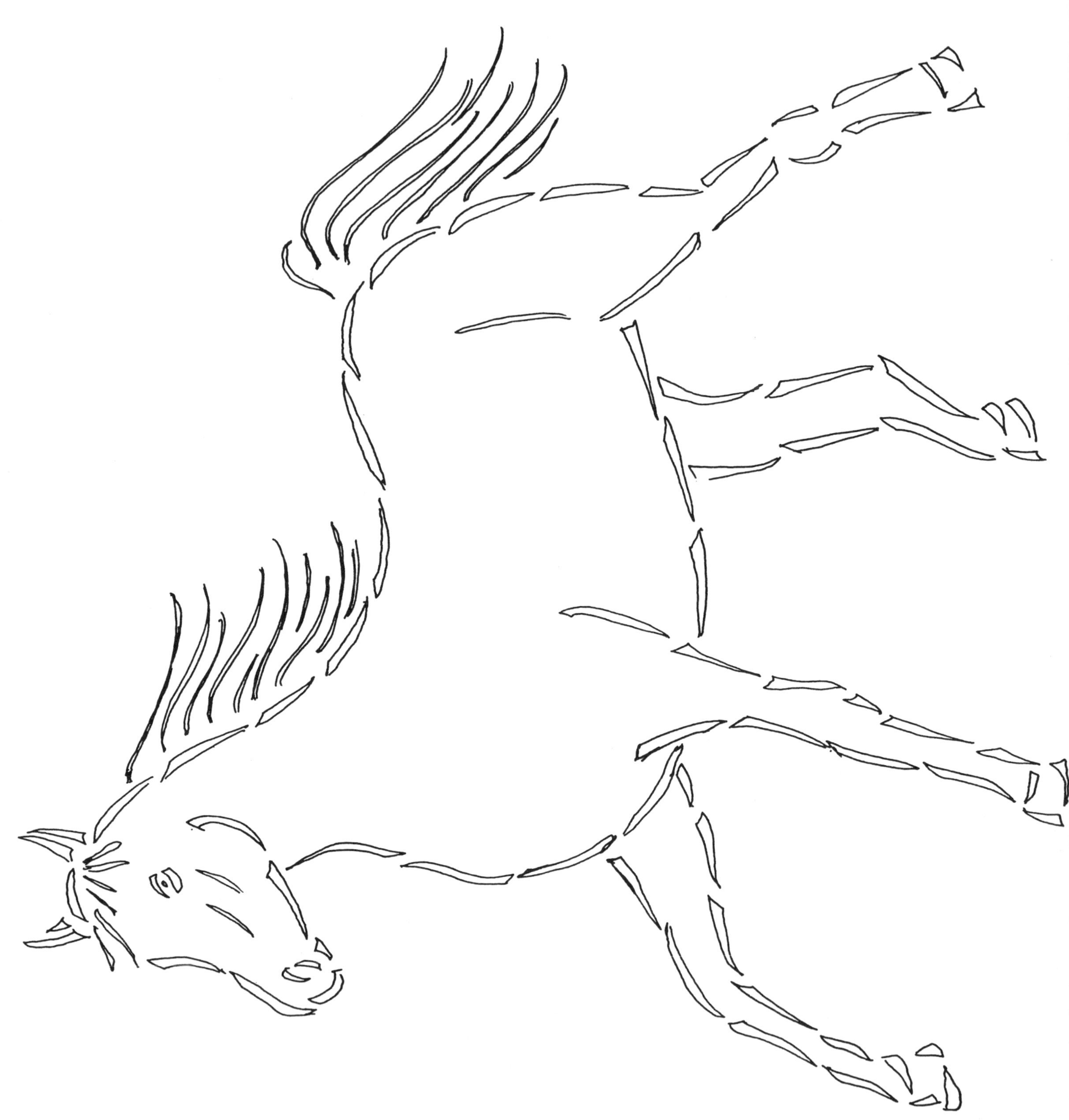

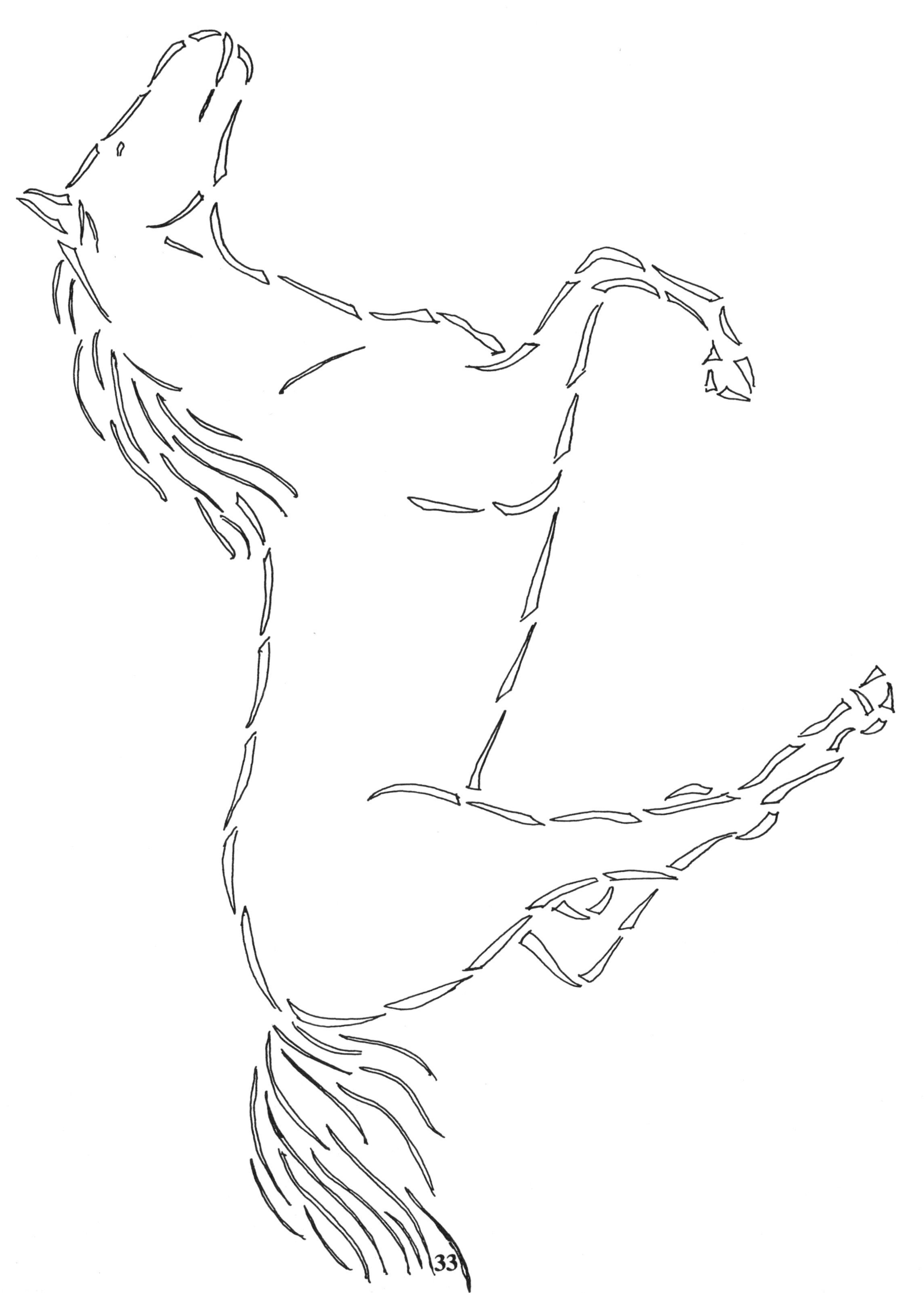

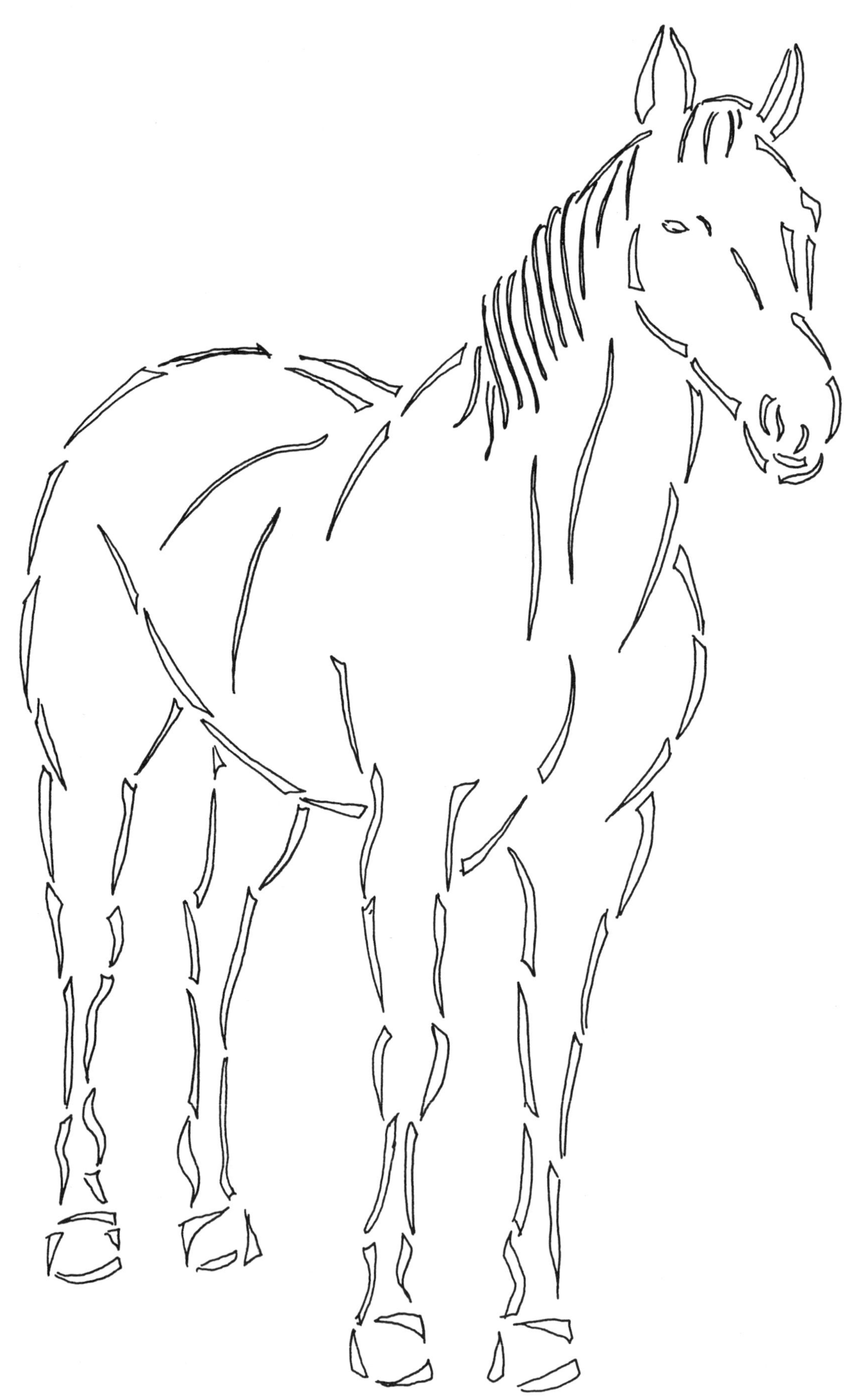

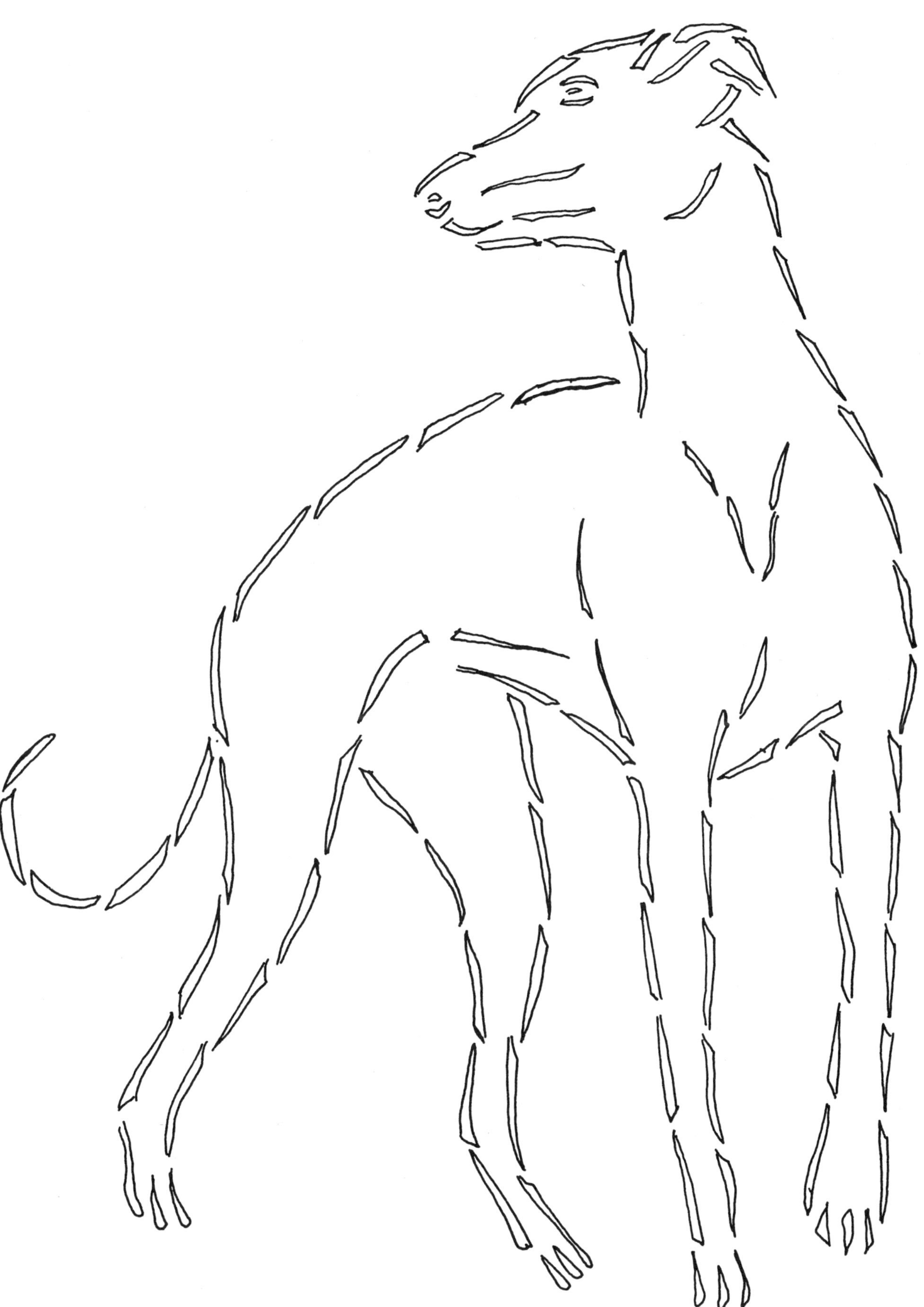

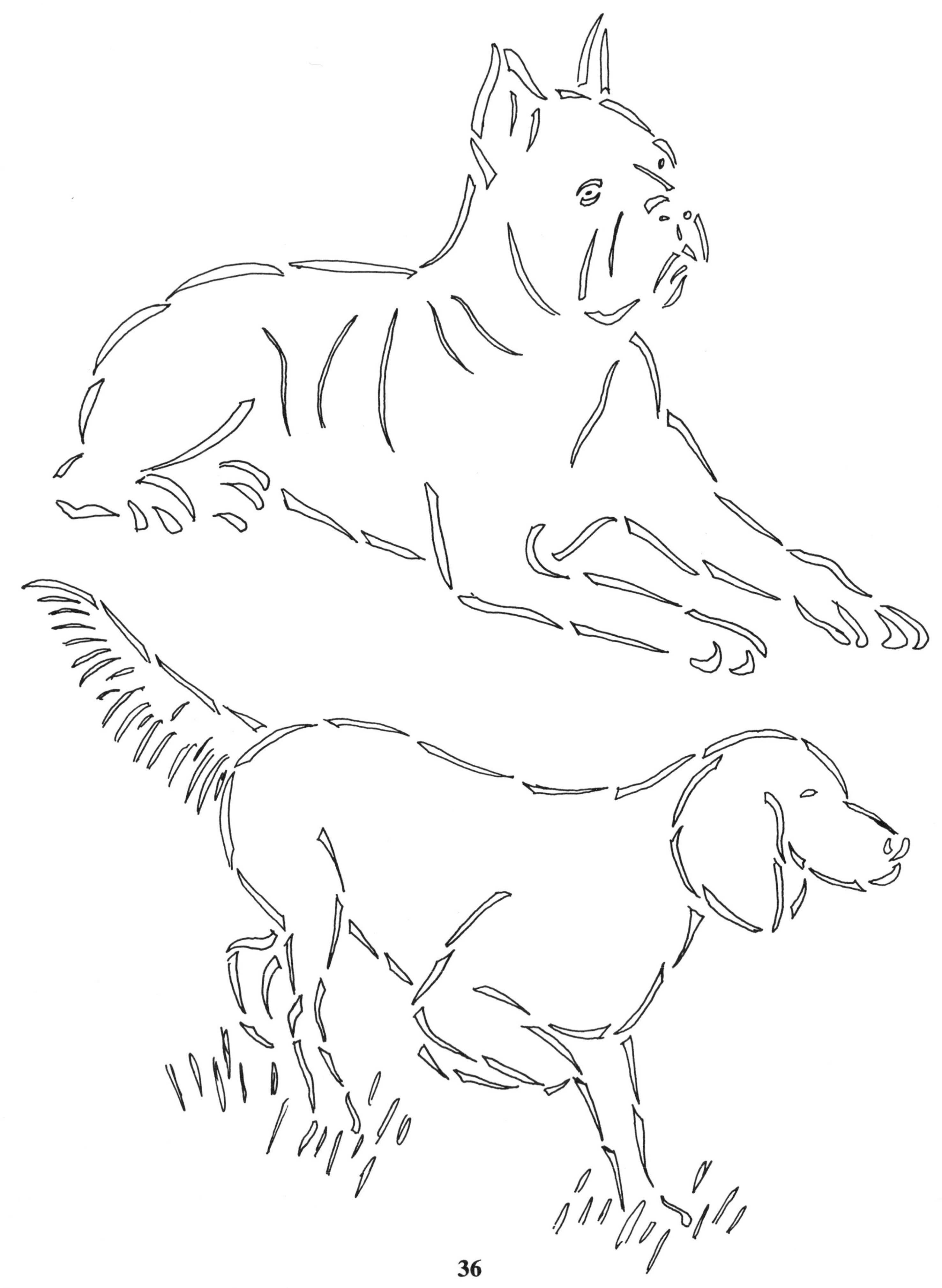

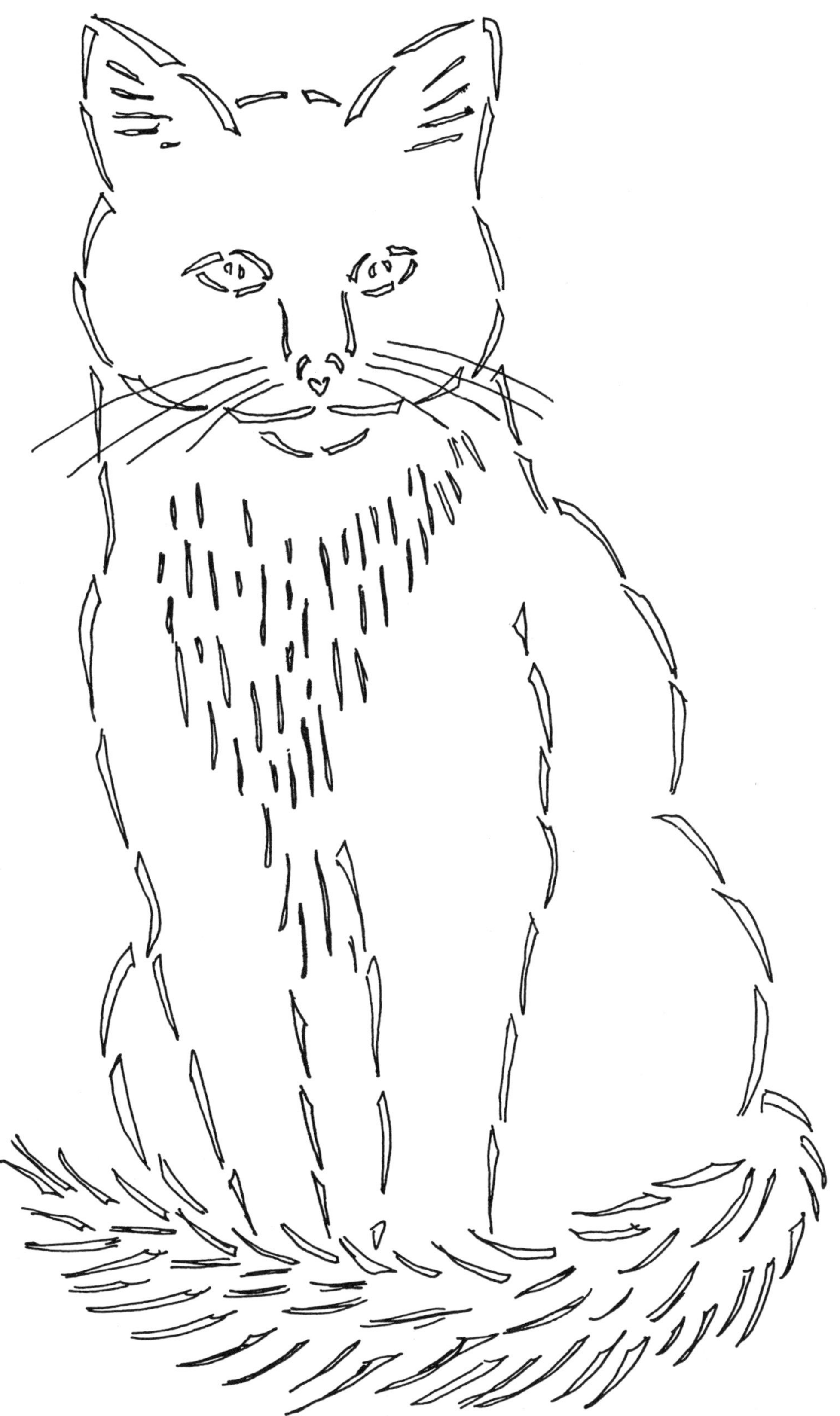

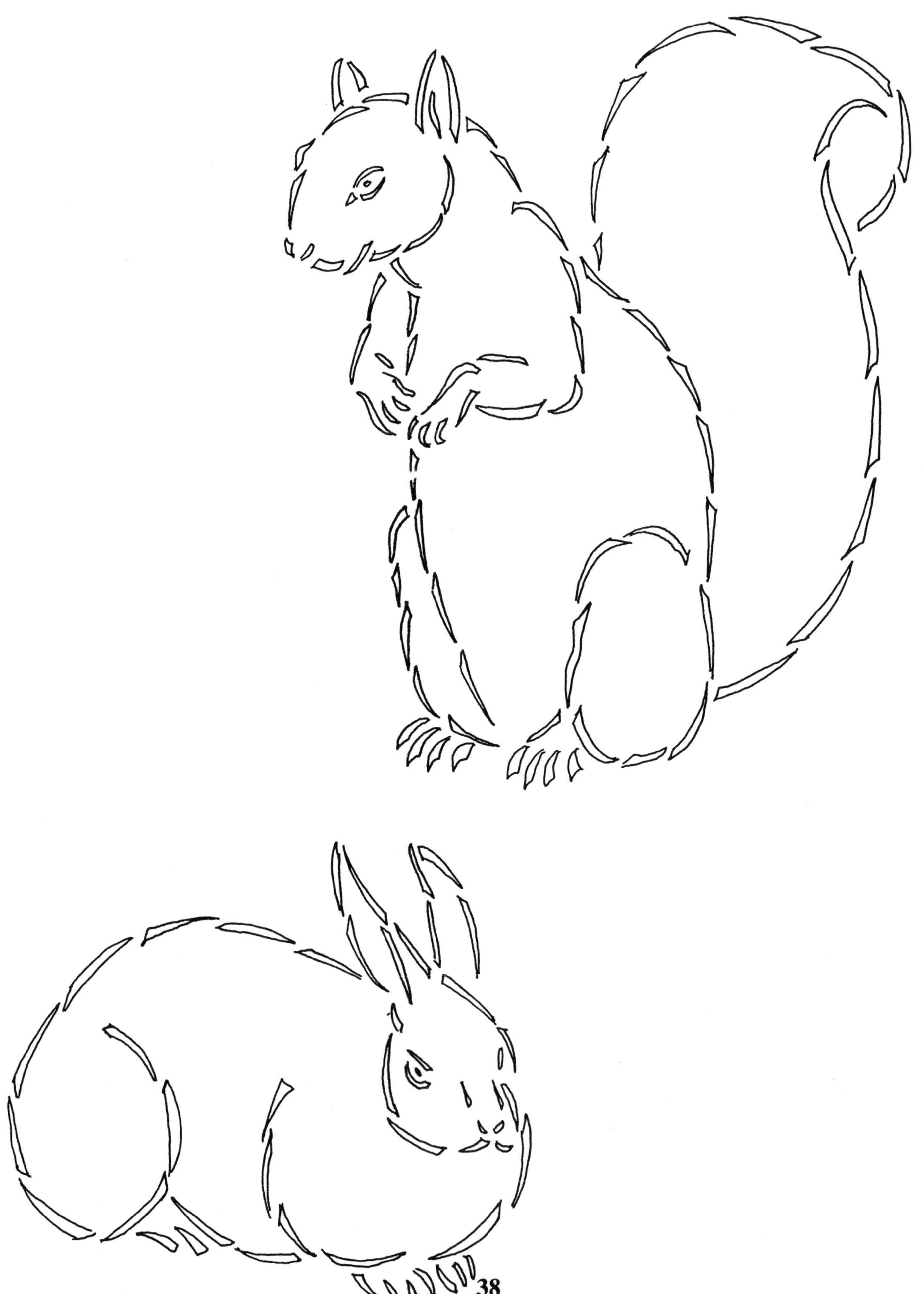

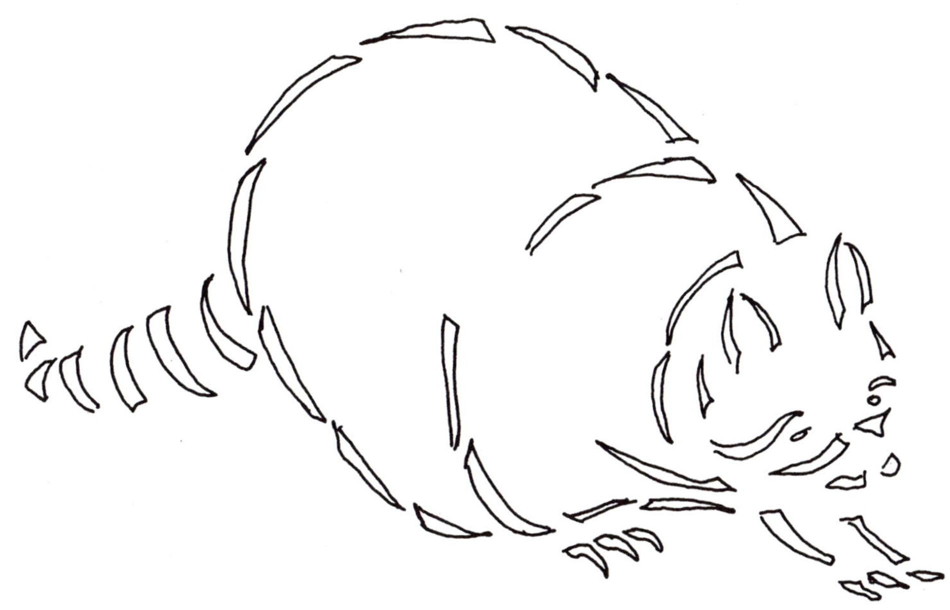

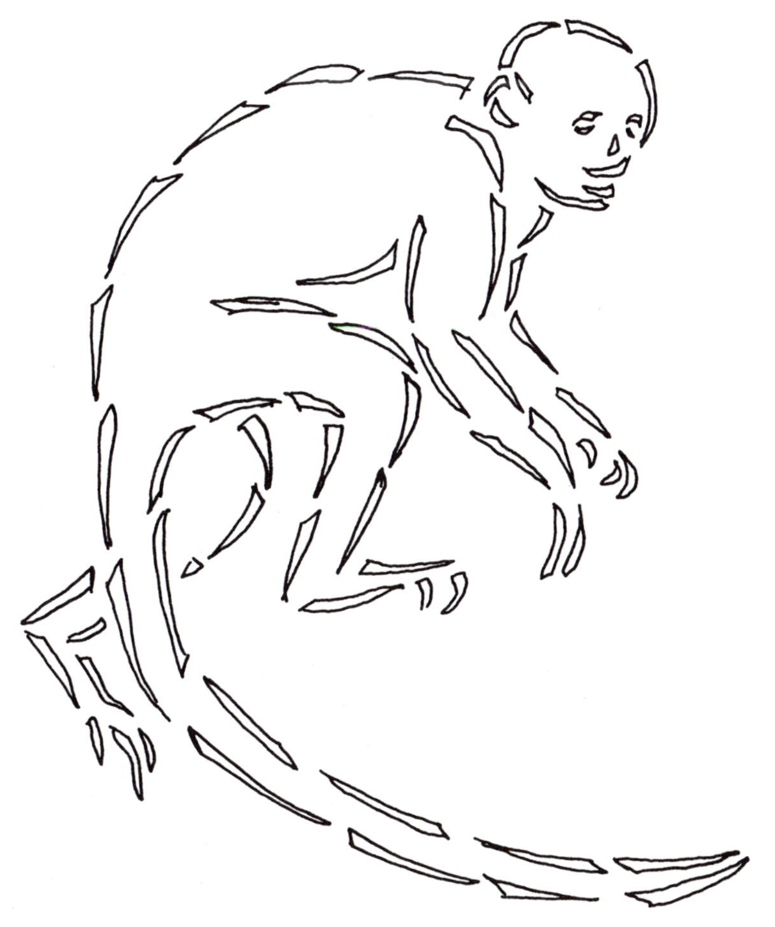

3 New Woodcarving Titles from Desiree Hajny

Big Cats: An Artistic Approach

Lions, tigers and jaguars... Oh my! In her second book in a series on carving mammals, renown wildlife carver Desiree Hajny shows you how to take a creative approach to carving the big cats of the savanah, the jungle and the rainforest. Close-up full color photographs of lions, tigers and jaguars in their natural habitat, detailed natural history notes, and anatomy charts provide you with the background information you'll need to *really* understand these beautiful bit cats. You'll even find study sketches from the artist's own notebook! Then focus in on techniques with a chapter devoted specifically to carving, burning and painting big cats. Comparative charts illustrate carving and burning techniques for legs, feet, eyes, ears, noses and mouths. Detailed pen-and-ink illustrations of the cats' fur show how to create the illusion of fur. Finally, follow Desiree as she demonstrates how to carve, burn and paint a miniature version of a lion. More than 90 full color photographs cover the entire process in spectacular detail.

Desiree even includes patterns for six big cat projects. Carve a lioness prowling while draped over a rock outcropping, or a tiger stepping quietly through the jungle. Two patterns featuring cubs—one of a cub with its mother's tail clamped playfully in its mouth and one of a cub being carried by its mother—are also included.

ISBN# 1-56523-071-X
Order Now! $14.95 retail

Carving Caricature Animals: An Artistic Approach

You won't be able to stop a smile from crossing your face as you take a look inside the world of animal caricature with carver Desiree Hajny. Through clearly written text and carefully drawn illustrations, Desiree teaches you how to focus in on the best features to caricature on any animal. Her artistic insight into caricature is balanced out by charts featuring carving techniques and a step-by-step demonstration on how to carve a lop-eared bunny with ears long enough to trip over. Use any one of her full-page charts on carving procedures to isolate the techniques for carving everything from eyes and ears to tails and feet. The step-by-step demonstration includes more than 50 full color photographs to guide you through the basics of caricature carving, burning and painting.

Desiree rounds out her book on caricature carving with eight ready-to-use caricature patterns featuring some of today's most popular animals. You'll find one of the most stubborn-looking mules around, laid-back bobcat, a spotted appaloose horse, a disappearing rabbit, a growling junk yard dog, and an otter doing the back float. She also includes instructions on how to alter these patterns to create endless animal caricatures of your choice.

ISBN# 1-56523-074-4
Order Now! $14.95 retail

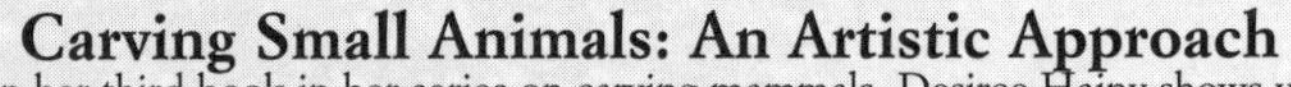

Carving Small Animals: An Artistic Approach

In her third book in her series on carving mammals, Desiree Hajny shows you an artistic approach to carving some of our favorite *smaller* mammals—specifically mischievous raccoons, cautious rabbits and acrobatic squirrels. You'll find reference photos showing these animals in their natural habitat, natural history notes, tips on how to conduct your own research and Desiree's own insights into the art of woodcarving. A chapter on technique addresses how to carve, burn and paint small animals. Clearly illustrated charts focus in on hard-to-carve areas, such as eyes, ears, noses and feet. She even shows you the basics of designing realistic small animal carvings through color-coded anatomical charts that show bone movement and weight distribution. A step-by-step demonstration with 85 full color photographs on carving, burning, and painting a standing cottontail—techniques that a carver can use on any small animal carving—completes this outstanding book on carving small animals.

Use the four patterns Desiree includes in her book to carve a raccoon family, a standing cottontail, a balancing gray squirrel or a red squirrel eating a nut. You can also alter these patterns using Desiree's detailed instructions to create new small animal patterns of your own.

ISBN# 1-56523-073-6
Order Now! $14.95 retail

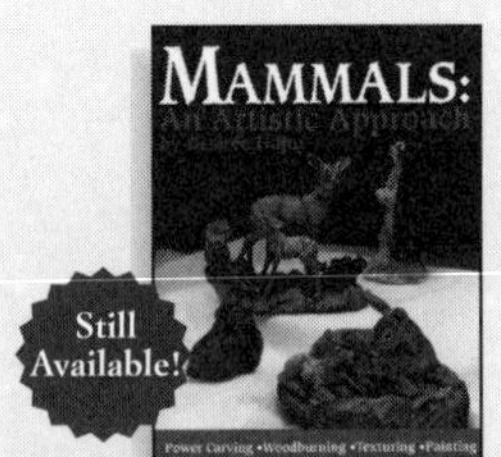

Mammals: An Artistic Approach

"Carvers will learn to carve realistic North American mammals–deer, bear and otters in this informative 150 page book. Techniques for both hand and power carvers are presented. Color painting section. Patterns plus much needed info on texturing and woodburning in the round."

ISBN #1-56523-036-1 $19.95

Available from your local bookstore or woodworking store, or by mail from the publisher. Please add $2.50 per book for postage.

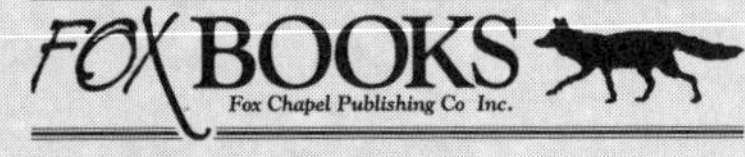

Fox Chapel Publishing Co., Inc.
PO Box 7948
Lancaster, PA 17604-7948

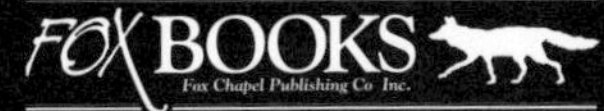

Titles From Fox Chapel Publishing

Desiree Hajny Titles

Big Cats by Desiree Hajny

NEW!

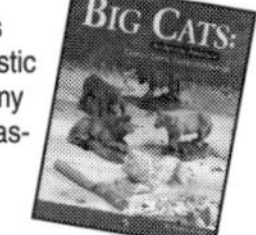

Carving Lions, Tigers and Jaguars. Desi's new full color guide to carving these majestic predators. 100's of color photos and anatomy charts guide you through creating your own masterpiece. Also features painting instructions and reference photos of live animals.

$14.95

Mammals:
An Artistic Approach
by Desiree Hajny (second printing)

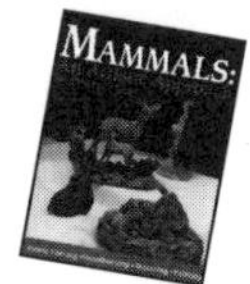

Carvers will learn to carve realistic North American mammals - deer, bear and otter in this informative 150 page book. Carving techniques for both hand tool and powercarvers are covered plus much needed info on texturing, woodburning and painting.
$19.95

Carving Caricature Animals by Desiree Hajny

NEW!

Learn how to make caricature carvings based on real animals. Desi shows you how to use cartooning techniques to emphasize an animal's most recognizable characteristics – and then turn those ideas into a caricature carving. Includes over 100 color photos, step-by-step carving and painting techniques, and patterns.

$14.95

Carving Small Animals

NEW!

In this comprehensive book, Desi includes everything you'll need to carve rabbits, racoons and squirrels. Anatomy sketches, descriptions of the animals, and reference photos give you a detailed look at your subject. Charts and photos outline techinques for carving and painting in a step-by-step fashion. Includes patterns, too!

$14.95

Mary Duke Guldan Titles

Mary Duke Guldan has been writing and illustrating the ìLets Carveî column here in Chip Chats for over a decade. The books below offer expanded and revised material.

Woodcarver's Workbook
Carving Animals with Mary Duke Guldan
Called the "best woodcarving pattern book in 40 years" by NWCA president Ed Gallenstein. Carving instructions and detailed information on 9 realistic projects including dogs, moose, wolves, whitetail deer, wild horses & more. **$14.95**

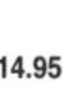

Woodcarver's Workbook #2
All new projects (no repeats from book #1 above). Projects inside: Native Indian Chief, buffalo, elk, horses, mules, cattle and oxen, plus a country farmer pattern.
$14.95

Caricature Carvers of America (CCA)

Carving The Full Moon Saloon
Caricature carvers will delight in the work of this group of great carvers. 21 members including well known teachers like Harold Enlow, Claude Bolton, Steve Prescott, Desiree Hajny, Tom Wolfe and Jack Price. Together, these members created "The Full Moon Saloon" a scale model measuring 4 feet long and containing over 40 carvings. Carving the Full Moon Saloon is a 120 page color guide to the creative work involved in these characters. Close up photos show incredible details. Includes patterns and painting technique section.

THE book for Caricature Carvers	**$19.95**
Hardcover edition (quantities limited)	**$29.95**

Steve Prescott Titles

Carving Blockheads by Steve Prescott
What is a Blockhead? A Blockhead is a basic shape roughout that can be carved into infinite character-filled personalities. Join Steve as he carves a basic blockhead and then features patterns and color photos of 50 more Blockheads - doctors, nurses, policeman, gnomes...and many more. An exciting new look at carving! **$12.95**

Cowtown Carving
Carving Characters with Texas Whittling Champion Steve Prescott.
15 projects including Cowtown Santa, Rodeo Clown and lots of cowboys! Steve includes both a full size bandsaw roughout pattern and a detail pattern for each project. Good pattern book for the intermediate + carver. **$14.95**

Whittling Old Sea Captain and Crew by Mike Shipley

NEW!

An exciting book on caricature style from this Ozarks Mountain carver. Over 100 photos and color painting guide plus patterns.

$12.95

Jim Maxwell Titles

Ozarks carver Jim Maxwell has been teaching and carving around Branson, MO for over 25 years. Jim's work shows clean lines, smooth finish and original patterns. Recently, we've started producing roughouts (see below) of his most popular projects.

Carving Clowns with Jim Maxwell
Over 200 b/w and color photos introduce you to the humorous world of clowns. Complete how to information for carving and painting. Patterns for 12 different clowns included inside. Highly Recommended! **$14.95**

Woodcarving Adventure Movie Characters
An excellent how to carve book using characters from Jim's favorite silver screen heroes as inspiration. Carve a sailor, cowboy or 21 other exciting characters. All patterns included inside.
Over 150 step-by-step photos. **$12.95**

Carving Characters
12 favorite projects including Jim's famous Turkey Buzzard.

$6.95

Making Collectible Santas and Christmas Ornaments
8 creative Santas and 34 ornament patterns. **$6.95**

Maxwell Roughouts
(#RO1) Roly Poly Santa (5") tall, **$6.00**
(#RO2) Snowman (4") tall, **$6.00**
(#RO3) Butterfly Catcher (Emmett Kelley-type) 10" tall, **$15.00**
(#RO4) Auguste - style - classic clown style 8" tall, **$15.00**

Bird Carving Titles

Carving Hummingbirds by Chuck Solomon and David Hamilton

NEW!

Full color guide to carving and painting "hummers". Patterns for broadtail and ruby throat included. 100's of photos in full color. Reference material on anatomy, wings and habitat.
Highly Recommended! **$19.95**

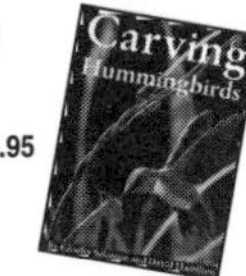

George Lehman Carving Pattern Books

Minnesota carver George Lehman's pattern books are a very useful source for beginning and intermediate carvers. Tips, sketches and techniques are sprinkled throughout each book. Four volumes available:

Book One:
Carving 20 Realistic Game and Songbirds
Partial list: common loon, chickadee, owl, mallard, grouse, robin, pintails.
$19.95

Book Two: Realism in Wood
Partial list: bald eagle, kingfisher, pheasants, bobwhite, great horned owl, pileated woodpecker, red-tailed hawk, mockingbird.
$19.95

Book Three: Nature in Wood
Partial list: barnswallow, cardinal, warblers (3), wrens, goldfinch + 10 animal patterns. **$16.95**

Book Four: Carving Wildlife in Wood
Partial list: Canada goose, wild turkey, osprey, Baltimore oriole, great blue heron. **$19.95**

Encyclopedia of Bird Reference Drawings by David Mohardt
Detailed sketches, wing studies and reference info for carvers. 215 different varieties of birds covered. Recommended by Larry Barth, Bob Guge.
$14.95

Carving Fish - Miniature Salt water and Freshwater by Jim Jensen
These detailed patterns, woodburning tips, color painting sections and step-by-step photos show you how to carve 26 different miniature fish for sale or display. **$14.95**

Carousel Horse Carving
An instruction workbook by Ken Hughes. Recommended as a classic how-to on carving carousel horses. Ken shows you everything step-by-step in making a denzel style carving in 1/3 standard size. Over 150 photos. New edition includes full size fold out pattern.

$24.95

Carving Vermont Folk Figures with Power
by Frank Russell, the Author of "Carving Realistic Animals with Power" offers an exciting collection of characters from The Bachelor to The Logger ready to use patterns included. **$9.95**

Fantastic Book of Canes, Pipes and Walking Sticks by Harry Ameredes
This WV Artist and carver has made canes simple and decorative for over 30 years. In these hundred of detailed drawings you'll find lots of ideas for canes, weathered wood and pipes. Plus info on collecting tree roots. **$12.95**

Bark Carving by Joyce Buchanan
Learn to harvest and carve faces - mystical woodspirits and other expressions in bark colorful guide with pattern and lots of helpful info.
$12.95

Sculpturing Totem Poles by Walt Way
Easy to follow pattern and instruction manual. Lots of clear drawings plus three patterns inside. **$6.95**

Carving Wooden Critters
Diane Ernst carves appealing animals that are best described as realistic caricatures. 16 high quality patterns for rabbits, puppies, otters and more. **$6.95**

Judy Gale Roberts Intarsia Books

Intarsia is a way of making picture mosaics in wood using 3/4" lumber. Carvers can further enhance their intarsia pieces by selective detailing.

Easy to Make Inlay Wood Projects
The best introduction to intarsia. Over 100 photos show you how it is done. Also includes 12 free patterns and 30 color photos.
$19.95

Small Intarsia Projects

NEW!

Full color guide with 12 patterns for a wide variety of pieces.
$14.95

300 Christian and Inspirational Designs

NEW!

Although written for scroll saw users, this book will be most helpful for carvers looking for designs to carve both in relief and in the round. **$14.95**

Mott Miniature Furniture Workshop Manual
Ready to use pattern for 144 scale model furniture projects.
Best book on the subject. **$19.95**

Toll Free 1-800-457-9112

How to order:

Credit card orders may call 1-800-457-9112

Mail orders please send book price plus $2.50 per book (maximum $5 shipping charge) to:

Fox Chapel Publishing
PO Box 7948 Lititz Pike
Lancaster, PA 17604-7948
FAX (717) 560-4702

Dealers write or call for wholesale listing of over 800 titles on woodworking and carving

NEW AND RECENT BOOK TITLES...

...from the experts!

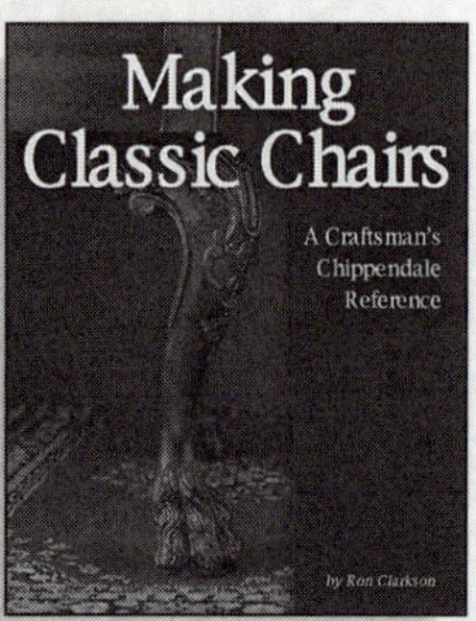

Making Classic Chairs:
A Craftsman's Chippendale Reference
Ron Clarkson & Tom Heller

188 pp. softcover
1-56523-081-7 **$24.95**

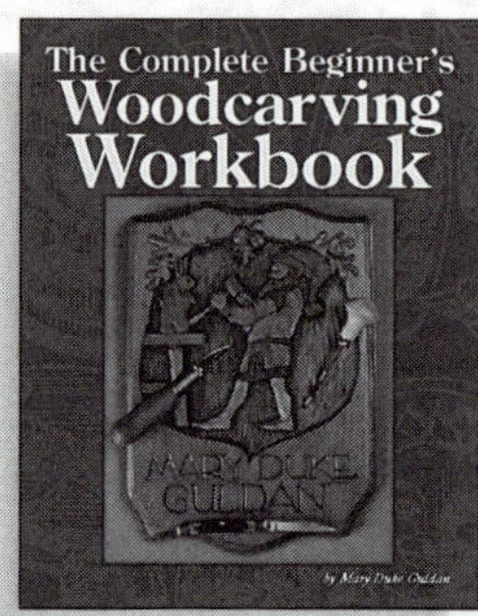

Complete Beginner's Woodcarving Workbook
Mary Duke Guldan

Softcover, 56 pages, 8.5 x 11
1-56523-085-X **$9.95**

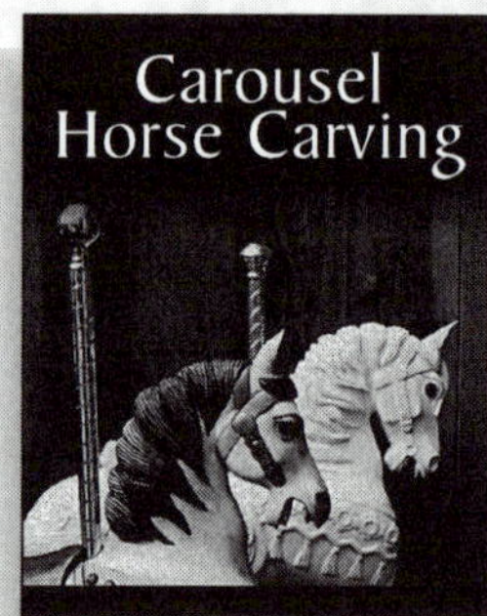

Carousel Horse Carving:
An Instructional Workbook in 1/3 scale
Ken Hughes

Perfect bound, color and black and white, how-to information, tool lists, full size pattern included.
1-56523-072-8 **$24.95**

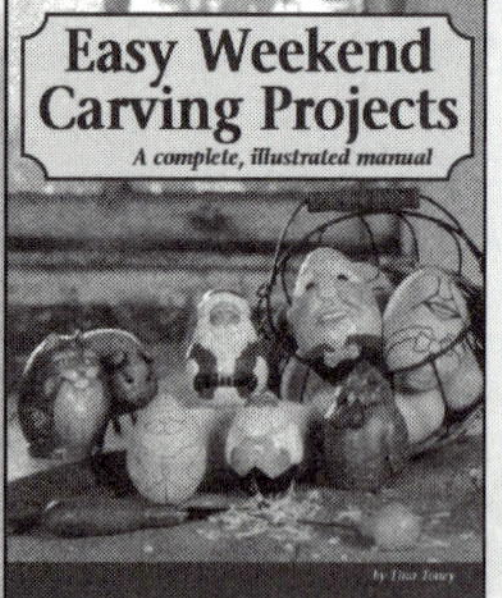

East Weekend Carving Projects
Tina Toney

56 pp. perfect bound, color and black and white, step-by-step carving and painting demonstrations patterns.
1-56523-084-1 **$12.95**

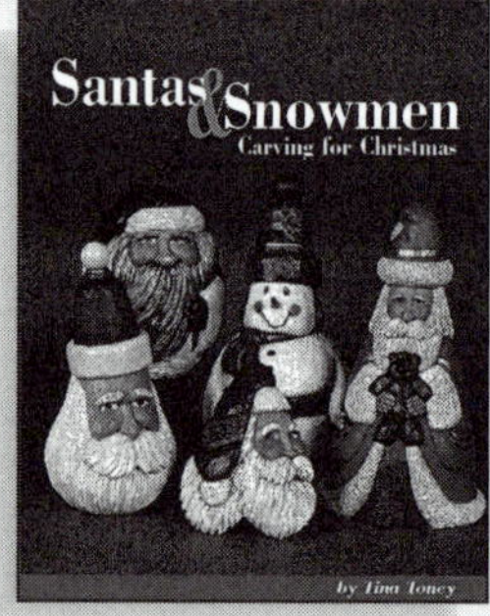

Santas and Snowmen:
Carving for Christmas
Tina Toney

56 pp. softcover, Full color.
1-56523-083-3 **$12.95**

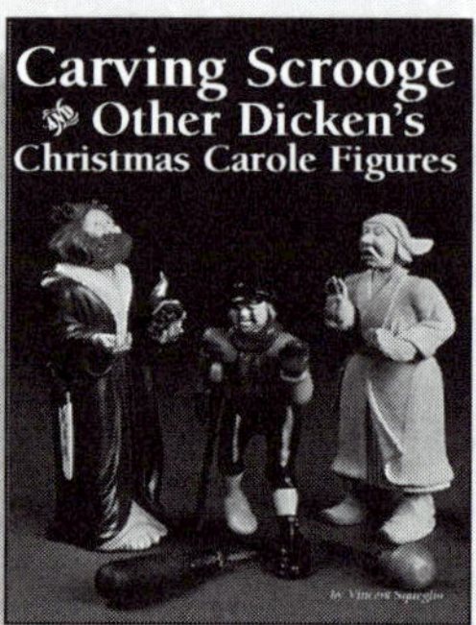

Carving Scrooge and Dickens's "A Christmas Carol"
(plus the Olde London Towne scene)
Vince Squeglia

56 pp. 10 complete patterns, full color gallery included.
1-56523-082-5 **$12.95**

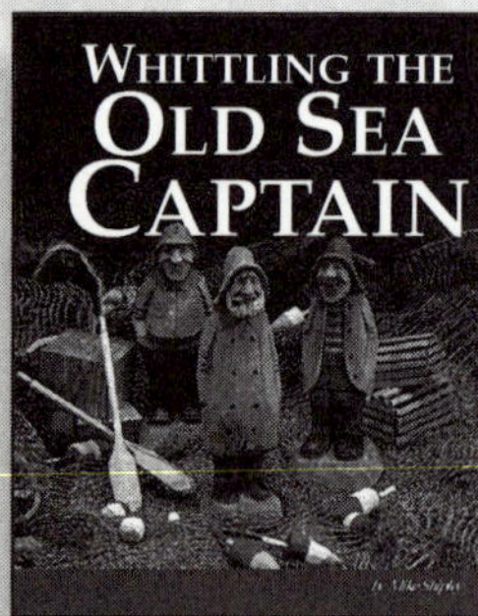

Whittling the Old Sea Captain
Mike Shipley

48 pp. perfect bound, color and black and white. Includes step-by-step carving & painting demonstrations, patterns, color photos of the finished captain crew.
1-56523-075-2 **$12.95**

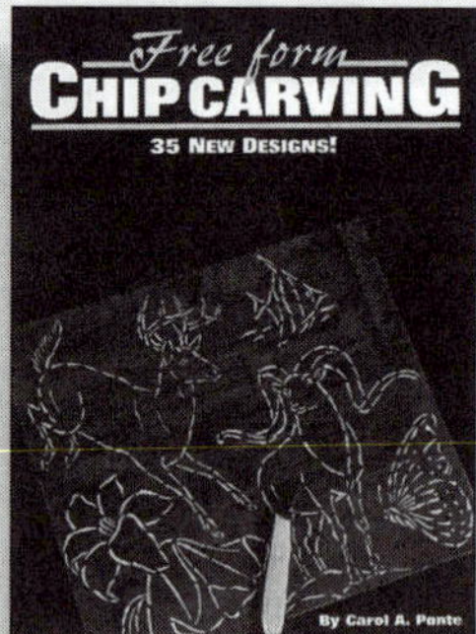

Free Form Chip Carving
Carol A. Ponte

48 pp. softcover
1-56523-080-9 **$7.95**

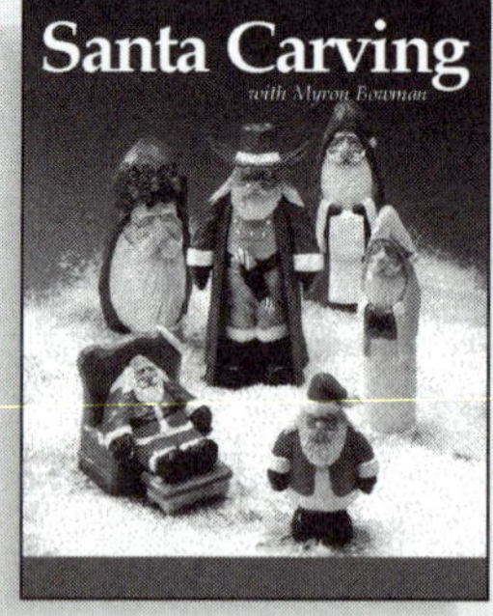

Santa Carving With Myron Bowman

56 pp. perfect bound, color and black and white. Includes step-by-step carving and painting demonstrations, 11 patterns, color photos of finished Santas.
1-56523-076-0 **$12.95**

FOX BOOKS
Fox Chapel Publishing Co Inc.

Fox Chapel Publishing Co., Inc.
PO Box 7948
Lancaster, PA 17604-7948

Ordering Information:
Try your favorite book supplier first!
Or see information on following pages to order direct from the publisher.